PRAUS
OF INDONESIA

PRAUS
OF INDONESIA

Clifford W. Hawkins

By the same author

The Dhow
A Maritime Heritage
Log of the Huia

ISBN 0 333 31810 2

First published 1982 by
NAUTICAL BOOKS
An imprint of Macmillan London Ltd
4 Little Essex Street
London WC2R 3LF

Associated companies in Auckland, Dallas,
Delhi, Dublin, Hong Kong, Johannesburg,
Lagos, Manzini, Melbourne, Nairobi,
New York, Singapore, Tokyo, Washington
and Zaria

Filmset by BAS Printers Limited, Over Wallop, Hampshire
Printed in Hong Kong by South China Printing Co.

Contents

Acknowledgements

In my quest for knowledge on the subject of *praus* I met Stephen Riley at the National Maritime Museum, Greenwich and it was he who introduced me to Warren Blake, another ardent *prau* enthusiast then resident in Singapore, and while at Singapore I visited Eric Alfred, curator of the Sentosa Maritime Museum. He brought to my notice the William Maxwell Blake photographs of *golekans* taken at Singapore many years before. I shall always be indebted to these kind folk who each in turn so imbued me with their own enthusiasm that I was determined to bring my own project to a successful conclusion. In this Erroll Bruce of Nautical gave me further encouragement by expressing his interest in the publication of a book on the Indonesian craft.

For making difficult research easier my thanks are extended to Ian Thwaites, librarian of the Auckland Institute and Museum, and to his staff; to the staff of the National Library of Australia and the Menzies Library of the University of Australia, both at Canberra. At Canberra, too, the hospitality afforded me by Adrian Horridge and his wife, Audrey, will be remembered as a kind act of Anzac friendship. I am also indebted to Australians Campbell Macknight and Howard Dick for their work on the *praus*.

For illustrations I wish to thank the Science Museum, London, for permission to use photographs made from the Blake negatives. David Brigham and Brian Leyland of Auckland and Brad Ives of the U.S.A. have also provided some very useful photographs. I am grateful too, to Caroline Hind of Nautical for her creative skill in arranging the illustrations and text.

Finally my good wishes are extended to Rahmat Ali on his appointment as *Direktur* of the Museum *Bahari* at Jakarta. It is my sincere hope that this museum will soon provide the historical background to the nearby Sunda Kelapa where the *praus* provide such a magnificent live panorama of sail.

C.W.H.

Introduction

By Basil Greenhill CMG BA FSA FRHistS
   Director National Maritime Museum, Greenwich

It is a pleasure to introduce Mr Hawkins' latest book. The text is in the long tradition of the descriptive recording by people of European origin of the vessels and boats of other cultures, but Clifford Hawkins has been more careful and thorough in his observations than some of the earlier field workers and the value of his text is greatly enhanced by the superb photographs, each of which conveys more than hundreds of words of description. The photographs in turn are complemented by the drawings.

I first met Clifford Hawkins in his home town of Auckland, New Zealand, in 1969, when he very kindly introduced me to other New Zealanders interested in maritime history matters. He also took me to see one of the very few survivors of the New Zealand *scows*, on which he is the leading authority. These were remarkable broad-beamed, flat-bottomed ketch or schooner rigged merchant sailing vessels which carried all their cargo on deck and drew no more water than the London river barge, but they sailed on the wild Tasman Sea.

Clifford and I had already been in correspondence for some years and I had read with great pleasure his books on New Zealand shipping, about the Tasman Sea schooner *Huia* and, in 'Out of Auckland', now re-issued with splendid illustrations as 'A Maritime Heritage', about the *scows* and New Zealand shipping generally.

But most of our letters were about quite different kinds of vessels. I had been fortunate in being able to study at first hand the multifarious local vessels of the great Brahma-putra river

system in what is now Bangladesh, and to publish some of the results of this field work. This work had caught Clifford Hawkins' attention and from him I learned of his own long involvement with the vessels of the Arabic speaking world and of his travels in the Persian Gulf and on the coasts of India. The results of this field work went into the making of 'The Dhow', one of the best books of its kind ever written, with some of the best photographs of Gulf and Arabian sea vessels ever taken.

But already Clifford Hawkins was thinking of another field, a natural extension of his travels and observations in the Muslim world—to the thousands of islands which make up Indonesia, where he worked among people perhaps nearer than the Arabs in outlook to my friends in Bangladesh. A few other Westerners have observed and described some of the vessels of this area, notably Adrian Horridge, whose work we at The National Maritime Museum have had the privilege of publishing.

Clifford Hawkins' book relates to this other work and gives us a comprehensive and positive view of Indonesian trade and the vessels engaged in it which can only fascinate and delight and which at the same time is a valuable contribution to the growing body of publications in the field of maritime ethnography.

Basil Greenhill

Preface

Having pursued the dhows throughout the Arabian Gulf and the Indian Ocean it seemed inevitable that, with an insatiable interest in sailing craft, I should eventually transfer my attention to the seas farther to the east where I knew there existed yet another stronghold of commercial sail. In Malaysia and the islands of Indonesia were the *praus* with an ancestral background similar to that of the dhows and whose antecedents were hardly known to Europeans even in the seventeenth century when adventurers who had penetrated to the 'Spice Islands' spoke of seeing *prawes* or *prauwes*. The name, in its diverse forms, continues in the journals of early navigators and of those who accompanied them. In 1770 Joseph Banks, aboard Cook's *Endeavour* at Batavia, wrote of the presence of numerous *proas*. Now, more than two centuries later, these vessels are still referred to as *perahus*, *proas* or *praus*.

In this work *prau* has been chosen as the spelling, not because it might have been used elsewhere but for the reason that it is very close to the word as spoken by the crew of the vessels. Repeatedly I heard it pronounced as 'prow-oo'. I was invited to go aboard a 'prow-oo' and the call came to photograph a 'prow-oo'. Never was it a *proa*. Here too I break away from the Bahasa Indonesian pluralising of the word by repetition whereby more than one *prau* is written as *prau prau* or *prau*². I have also kept Indonesian names to a minimum because they differ in various islands or even in a single locality where different linguistic groups exist. *Layar*, for instance, although it is of Malay origin, is known throughout Indonesia as the word for 'sail' but in South Sulawesi the Konjo word is *sombala*; the Bugis, *sompé*; and Mandar, *sobal*. It can all become very complicated and confusing for a stranger to these waters. I shall, however, use the Konjo/Bugis word *pinisi* for ketch, and certain other local names where it might be advantageous to do so.

English literature concerning the *prau* is not prolific. There are the illustrated articles of George Ernest Patrick Collins that appeared in the English *Geographical Magazine* in 1937 and in the American *National Geographic* in 1945. Collins was also the author of *East Monsoon* and *Makassar Sailing* but since their publication in 1937 great changes have taken place in what was then known as the Netherlands East Indies. Makassar has reverted to the name Ujung Pandang (the point of a sacred leaf) and the island of Celebes to Sulawesi, while the Batavia of the Dutch is again Jakarta. But more than name changes have occurred since the Indies became the Republic of Indonesia and in the maritime field one of the most remarkable advances has been the tremendous growth of the *prau* trade and the number of vessels that take part in it.

The equivalent of James Hornell's dhow classification (see Bibliography) must be the Admiralty publication *Fishing and Trading Craft of the Netherlands East Indies, New Guinea, etc.* which was produced as a 'classified' work in 1944. That, with the papers of C. A. Gibson-Hill which appeared in the *Journal of the Malayan Branch of the Royal Asiatic Society* in 1949–50

The Sulawesi *prau patorani Bulan Purnama*.

Praus at Jakarta's Sunda Kelapa.

provide a valuable background to the archaeology and distribution of the various types of Malaysian and Indonesian *praus*. But more recently some newcomers have made valuable contributions to our *prau* literature and it was my pleasure to meet only recently (1979) Adrian Horridge, Campbell Macknight and Howard Dick, all of Australia.

When refering to any of the published material that deals with *praus* it is essential to take note of the period to which the information is relative, more especially because, since our first acquaintance with these craft, changes have progressively taken place in both hull and rig. Some types of *prau* no longer exist while others have so altered that they bear little resemblance to their namesake predecessors. Hybrids have also developed as the result of Chinese and Malaysian infiltration and the influence of European shipbuilding practice. The *prau* trade too is certainly far from being static and it is quite obvious that many more and much larger *praus* than ever before are now in commission.

It might be disputed as to what craft may rightly be termed as *praus* especially as they are known to range in size and type from the small fishing canoes or *koleks* to the big *pinisi* trader.

Generally speaking all sailing vessels other than small inshore craft are eligible for the entitlement. It is difficult to draw a line. Some are classified by the sails they carry so that we have the *leti-leti* with its oceanic lateens; the Sulawesi *prau patorani* with *sombala tanja* or tilted 'square' sails; and the *nadé* with its European-type sloop rig. Then there are names that specifically refer to the hull; *lambok* if it is European in nature and having gaff rig; *sekoci* if it is a double-ended indigenous hull with gaff rig; and *leti-leti* for a double ender with lateen sails. However, there may be other local names for some of these *praus*, depending on where they hail from, but there is little point in becoming involved with them here. Enough said perhaps that the name *pinas* or *pinisi* is derived from the European pinnace, or pinasse, a two masted vessel that was employed in the Indies in earlier times.

It has been said that the high poop and the square transom stern, as in the Bugis *palari*, was copied from the Portuguese traders of the sixteenth century. It must be remembered, however, that the Chinese junks with their ungainly stern galleries and other structural peculiarities penetrated beyond the South China Sea long before the arrival of European vessels in these waters. The projecting poop or *ambeng* as seen in the *praus* throughout Malaysia and Indonesia is just as likely to have developed through a relationship with the Chinese traders rather than by the influence of European ship design. Then too the Chinese battened lugsail has been very much in evidence in Malaysian *praus* and in the Singapore trader. In the Indonesian craft, though, the European fore-and-aft rig is more general. The indigenous tilted 'square' sail, however, is still to be seen, especially in South Sulawesi, and the oceanic lateen is also prevalent, in the Madura *leti-leti* for example.

Of the various types of *prau* in the Java Sea area the *pinisi* is the most prominent as a trader. It has developed from the *palari*, a smaller craft that was built in South Sulawesi, particularly at Bira, and sailed by the Bugis seafarers. Today many of the *palari's* successors are quite large vessels of quasi-European rig capable of stowing some 200 tonnes of cargo. These are the *praus* that are so often seen from overseas merchant ships while on passage through the Java Sea.

I have recollection of a film which portrayed a Bugis family of traders, several generations of whom had sailed in and owned *praus* out of Tanjung Perak, the port of Surabaya. Male members of this enterprising family grow up right from birth in an atmosphere of maritime trade and at an early age a boy has already become familiar with a business life, running messages ashore, and has been voyaging in a *prau*. He then receives training in various branches of the family business before taking a responsible position that could range from that of *prau nakhoda* to directorship. This family, the Hasans of Surabaya, in 1974, owned nine *pinisi praus* of which the newest had then just been commissioned with great ceremony and feasting. And what a glorious sight the *Maminasae* made as she approached Tanjung Perak deeply laden with Kalimantan teak from Banjarmasin.

At Jakarta's Kali Baru I was befriended by a youth from a '*Prau Layar Motor*' who took me along narrow alleys and past stacks of timber to his family's office. He was very proud to introduce me to the *Direktur* whose position he would probably succeed to in years to come.

Due to the geographic orientation of Indonesia voyages made by *praus* must be governed to a great extent by the seasonal east–west changes of the air stream. On perusing a chart it is seen that the 13,667 Indonesian islands[1] spread over some forty degrees of East longitude. This can quite easily involve three thousand sea miles of sailing with a fair wind on a voyage commencing at the north-west extremity of Sumatra and continuing through the Malacca Strait to the south-east into the Java Sea with Kalimantan to port and Bangka to starboard. Then heading more toward the east, past Sulawesi and, avoiding the shoals of the Flores Sea, the Banda Sea is reached with the island of Ceram to the north until finally Irian Jaya prevents any further progress north-eastward. This distant shore, together with the Aru Islands (Kepulauan Aru), defines the eastern limit of Indonesian *prau* trade. The voyage detailed, however, is one not likely to be made and it encompasses the chart only in a west–east direction. The *praus* deviate in every conceivable course according to their trade and the season. They are just as familiar with the Makassar Strait as they are with the waters to the east of Sulawesi.

Throughout Indonesia the two seasons which affect the *praus* are monsoonal. They are the periods when the north-west and the south-east winds are prevalent. With those three thousand odd sea miles from north-west Sumatra to the coast of Irian Jaya and more than a thousand miles between the major ports of Tanjung Priok in Java and Ujung Pandang in Sulawesi it is quite obvious that in order to make the voyage a *prau* must sail with the monsoonal wind rather than against it. It would therefore be correct to assume that the south-east wind would carry many of the *praus* to the ports in the west of Indonesia. There is also the seasonal trek of those returning to the eastern area, particularly South Sulawesi, with the strength of the north-west monsoon at the end of the year. Many of the *praus*, on arrival at their home port or *kampong*, are hauled out for a short laying up period and overhaul. Those proposing to make a voyage east to the Banda Sea must leave the Java Sea before the westerly dies and in time to reach their destination, whether it be distant Ambon, the Aru Islands or Irian Jaya, to catch the beginning of the easterly wind for the return journey.

The long voyages of former years are not so likely to be made by *praus* nowadays as motor vessels have taken over much of

the long distance trade. The sailing *praus* are now more likely to keep to certain overlapping areas rather than make the long trading voyages they once did. Even so some of the voyages made by present-day Indonesian *praus* must be among some of the longest undertaken by any commercial sailing craft now in commission. During the peak of the sailing season the Java, Flores and Banda Seas are criss-crossed with the tracks of *praus* under sail as they make their way with all manner of trade.

The ideal scheduling for a season's trading would be to make a departure from Southern Sulawesi for the eastern islands at the tail end of the west monsoon by the end of March, then head back to Java as the wind sets in from the east. With some intermediate voyaging in the Java Sea the crew could then look forward to returning home with a favourable wind by December. Short transitional periods occur in the weather between the two major seasons. In the months of April and

November the winds are light and variable so that any voyage undertaken then could be somewhat protracted because of frustrating conditions.

My visits to Indonesia took place between the months of July and September with the prevailing wind coming from the south-east. This brought many of the *praus* into the ports of Java and would continue to do so for some time, a circumstance that fortunately always coincides with the most pleasant season in which to linger in these parts; and this is a most important consideration. In October the 'wet season' begins to set in and the north-west monsoon brings heavy rain between November and March. The south-east monsoon is the 'dry season' lasting from April through to October. During the transitional periods of April and November frequent thunder storms take place. So, as with the dhows in the Arabian Sea, the voyaging of the *praus* is dependent on the seasons.

Cliff Hawkins

Right: At Ujung Pandang, Sulawesi.

Left: A Madura *leti-leti* making for Semarang.

Indonesia

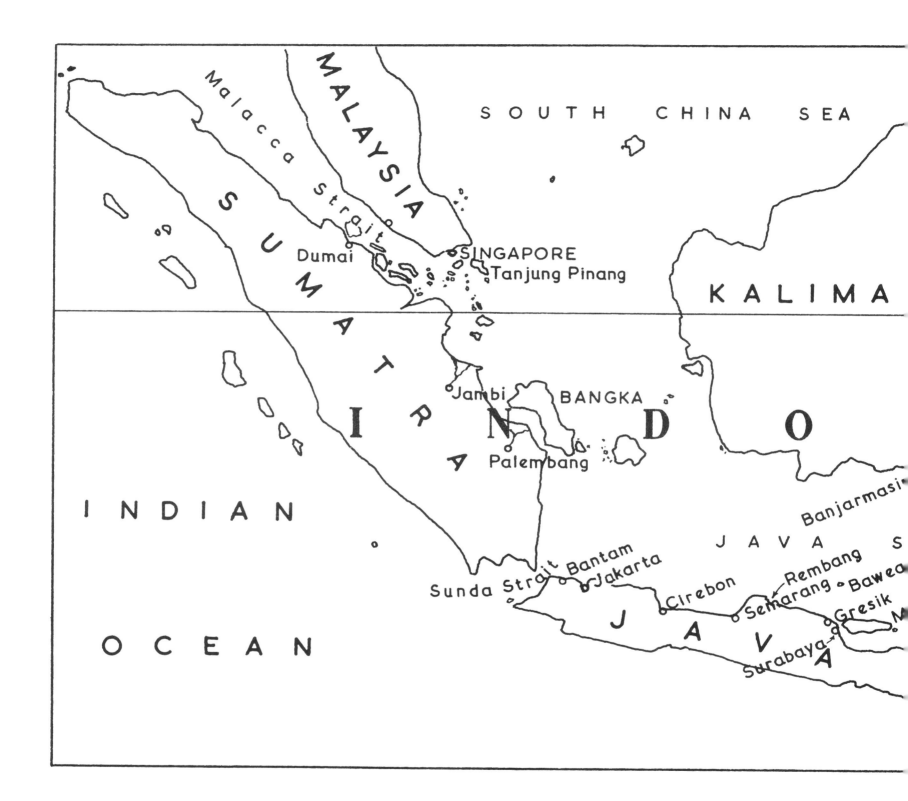

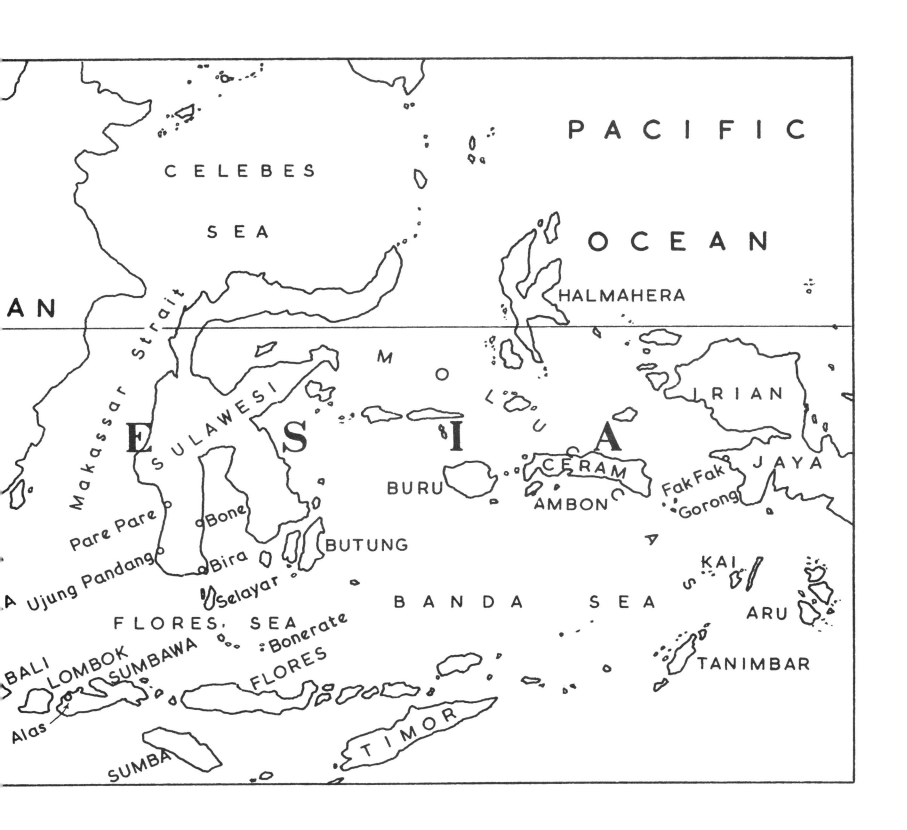

PACIFIC

OCEAN

CELEBES

SEA

HALMAHERA

AN

Makassar Strait

M

O

L

U

C

C

A

IRIAN

SULAWESI

E

S

I

A

JAYA

BURU

CERAM

FakFak

Pare Pare

Bone

AMBON

Gorong

Ujung Pandang

Bira

BUTUNG

KAI

Selayar

BANDA   SEA

ARU

FLORES   SEA

TANIMBAR

BALI

LOMBOK   SUMBAWA

Bonerate

FLORES

Alas

TIMOR

SUMBA

Jakarta (Tanjung Priok main deep-sea harbour. Kali Besar at Sunda Kelapa and Kali Baru *prau* harbours).

Surabaya (Tanjung Perak deep-sea harbour. Kali Mas *prau* harbour).

Praauwen, Eylant Amsterdam, circa 1700. From *Oost Indien*, Francois Valentyn, courtesy Auckland Institute and Museum. Valentyn, a Lutheran minister, was born in Dordrecht and arrived in Batavia in 1686. Initially he spent twelve years in the Moluccas and a second spell of seven years duration terminated in 1714. His monumental work was published in several volumes between 1724 and 1726.

The twin-hulled craft has a long outrigger boom but the vang from the head of the yard to the end of this boom is not shown. The lower yard or boom of the oceanic lateen sail is also missing.

Dwelling on the Past

Navigation throughout the Indonesian seas always has been frought with danger. Extensive coastal shallows and coral reefs as well as strong currents must all be taken into consideration when making a voyage, with local knowledge contributing very much to its success. A *nakhoda* knows that he must take advantage of the monsoonal winds in order to make a long ocean passage but to sail through a strait between any of the numerous islands or to work along a coast he also has to make use of the land and sea breezes.

European ship masters soon learned how to bring a voyage to the East Indies to a successful conclusion by observing the *praus* off Java Head and on through the Sunda Strait to Batavia. From about midnight, during the east monsoon, a *prau* took advantage of the land breeze to be carried along the Java coast although in doing this she would unavoidably gradually increase her distance from the land. Soon after sunrise, with the wind coming in from the east, further progress in the direction of Batavia would temporarily become impossible so, to prevent drifting back on the current, the anchor was dropped until the sea breeze set in some time about noon. Then the anchor was raised and the *prau* was able to make her way back to the land. Again the anchor was dropped until the land breeze reappeared in the middle of the night. This was a comparatively simple procedure in a *prau* but a backbreaking task in a square-rigged East Indiaman.

In 1865 Albert Bickmore, travelling through the 'East Indian Archipelago', observed in the roadstead at Makassar (Ujung Pandang) 'many praus of forty or fifty tons' burden, and some even twice as large. In the beginning of the west monsoon they go in great numbers to the Arru (Aru) Islands, the principal rendezvous for the people of Ceram, Goram (Gorong), the Ki (Kai) Islands, Tanimber (Tanimbar), Baba (Babar) and the adjacent coast of New Guinea'. Two of the Makassar *praus* were seen at Port Essington on the Coburg Peninsula of Australia's Northern Territory some years previously (January 1845). 'One had made the passage from Macassar in ten, and another in fifteen days. But', said Bickmore, 'on these long voyages, many never return. In the last of the month a third came into that port and reported that four others, more than had arrived safely, had just foundered during a heavy gale, and that the crew of only one was saved'. Some of the *praus* voyaged to Papua (Irian Jaya) and even ventured right round to Geelvink Bay on the north-east coast.

Bickmore considered that those long voyages indicated that the Bugis sailors were then what the Malays were at the time when the Portuguese first came to the East; the great navigators and traders of the archipelago. To all of the previously mentioned places the *praus* took English calicoes and native-manufactured cottons. Chinese gongs and large quantities of arrack were also shipped. Return cargoes consisted of tortoise-shell (actually turtle), mother-of-pearl, pearls, birds of paradise and trepang. Of the latter, near fourteen thousand piculs (1 picul = 132 lbs) were shipped from Makassar each year valued at almost six hundred thousand dollars.

Contemporary with Bickmore's account of trade between Makassar and the eastern islands is that of Alfred Wallace, F.R.G.S. He was in the area during the first six months of 1857 and read a paper on his travels at a Royal Geographic Society meeting the following year. Just prior to the visit of Wallace some of the northern islands had been terrorised by New Guinea pirates. Consequently the geographer's investigations

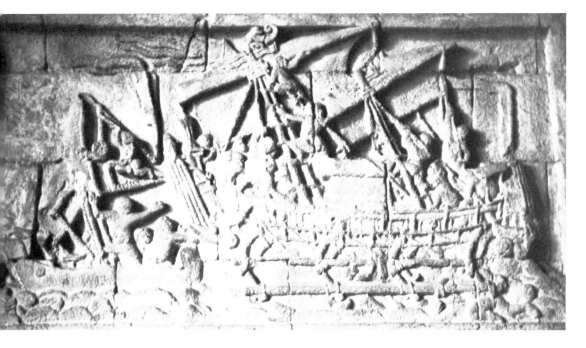

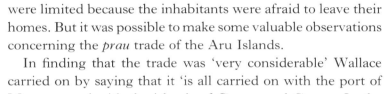

were limited because the inhabitants were afraid to leave their homes. But it was possible to make some valuable observations concerning the *prau* trade of the Aru Islands.

In finding that the trade was 'very considerable' Wallace carried on by saying that it 'is all carried on with the port of Macassar and with the islands of Goram and Ceram. In the present year (1857) fourteen large prows, of from fifty to one hundred tons, and one brig arrived at Dobbo from Macassar. The owners are Bugis, Chinese or Dutch, and the gross value of their cargoes about 20,000 l. Besides these, not much short of two hundred boats and prows of small size arrived from Ke, Goram and Ceram, the whole value of whose cargoes may be 7,000 l or 8,000 l more. The Macassar traders bring rice, tobacco, gamber, muskets, brass cannon, gunpowder, gongs, swords, knives, choppers, axes, English and Chinese crockery, calicoes and cottons, Bugis cloth and arrack. The prows from Goram and Ceram bring principally sago-cakes, which are there manufactured for the supply of all the eastern part of the archipelago. The Ke islanders bring boats and prows for sale, wooden bowls, native earthen vessels, cocoa-nuts, and plantains. The produce obtained consists of pearl-shell, pearls, tripang birds'-nests, and I believe most of the pearls and tortoise-shell find their way to China, the mother-of-pearl shell principally to Europe.

Each of the larger prows calls at Ke on its way to Aru, and purchases there one or two small vessels, which are loaded immediately on arriving, and sent with a supercargo to pick up produce among the islands on the east coast. The traders themselves reside at Dobbo, where they all have houses built entirely of poles and palm-thatch, and annually repaired. Natives from all the adjacent parts daily arrive, bringing their

little bits of produce, which they sell to the highest bidder. They may often be seen wandering about with a single pearl shell, calling at every house to see where they can get the highest price. These as well as the tripang (sic), tortoise-shell, and birds'-nests, are all bought by weight; and a whole cargo is made up by purchases of a few pounds or even a few ounces at a time. When a native has accumulated a little stock of produce, he takes payment in an assortment of articles, including always a box of arrack, the quantity of which consumed is immense. About 3,000 boxes are brought annually, each containing fifteen square bottles of very near half a gallon each, making a total of about 20,000 gallons of strong spirit.

The prows begin to arrive at Dobbo in December, at the commencement of the west monsoon; and in June and July they return to Macassar. Some of the small traders remain the year round, picking up produce at a greater profit when there is less competition; and some of the larger merchants leave agents to do the same for them.'

Wallace remarked that the profits from the Aru trade had fallen due to excessive competition. Remarkably, English calicoes could be had in Aru as cheap as in England.

For comparison it is worth including here an account of a season's trading made by a Bugis *palari* three quarters of a century later[2]. The *prau* left Bira, her home *kampong* in Sulawesi, on 3 April 1935 with the west monsoonal wind in her favour. No cargo was on board and within two weeks the islands to the north-west of Fak Fak, on what is now Iran Jaya, had been reached. There the crew collected bark and by the end of the month were ready to depart with the setting in of the easterly weather. The north coast of Ceram would have been skirted on the way to Buru where water was taken in and on to

Butung for more water, and firewood. Further calls were made during the long haul to Java and Gresik was reached on 9 July; and the bark sold.

From Gresik the *prau* sailed for Alas on the north-west coast of Sumbawa to load rice and by mid-August was bound for Bawean in the Java Sea. On arrival there the cargo was immediately discharged and, wasting no time, a departure was made that very same day for another trip to Sumbawa. A call was made at Madura for water and, reaching her destination in good time, rice was loaded at two different places and by the end of September the *prau* was again making for Java, this time Surabaya which was reached on 5 October. On discharging the rice a general cargo was accepted for Jakarta, a journey that concluded after almost three weeks at sea. With October drawing to a close and the return of the north-west monsoon the *prau* sailed empty, once more for Sumbawa, arriving at Alas on 20 November. Again rice was loaded, this time for the home *kampong* of Bira and so, in just under a week, the season's trading came to an end.

Throughout the centuries of foreign trade in the 'Indian Archipelago' fortunes have changed many times. Long before the Portuguese established direct trade with Malacca the Chinese were carrying silks and porcelain ware to the Straits port for transhipment to India and beyond by Arab dhows. They were also sending their junks to Riau which enjoyed a large measure of foreign trade and the export of tin from the mines in Bangka. The junks sailed even further, to Makassar and the Moluccas.

When the European ships penetrated the Strait of Malacca the pattern of trade changed rapidly. Banten, in Java, during the sixteenth century became a 'factory' of the Portuguese but that was eventually displaced by the Dutch when they created Batavia at Sunda Kelapa. The Dutch East Indiamen from Europe usually terminated their outward voyages at Batavia and local craft, many of them Dutch owned, and *praus*, carried out the inter-island trade and conveyed the valuable spice cargoes from the Moluccas, Celebes (Sulawesi) and Sumatra. Tanjung Pinang on Bintan (Kepulauan Riau) to the south-east of the Strait of Malacca prospered as a Malay entrepôt port during the eighteenth century. The Bugis people had a toehold there until the Dutch evicted them in 1784. To counter the Dutch incursion and the consequent loss of trade and in fear of the Bugis going elsewhere the Malays proposed developing Malacca but before any action could be taken the British had attracted much of the Riau trade to Penang.

Riau had been a great centre for the traffic in opium but more important was the trade in tin from the Bangka mines. It was shipped to China in junks and to India in European vessels, some on their return from China. Pepper came to Tanjung Pinang from Palembang, Jambi and other Sumatran ports, and from Kalimantan. English and Portuguese ships brought in cotton trade goods from India and the junks brought Chinese manufactured goods. There was also a vast exchange of trade with other South-east Asian countries.

The foreign trade provided the Malay and Bugis seafarers with much of their livelihood as a considerable amount of the cargoes brought in to the main centres of overseas trade went out to the lesser islands in *praus* which also freighted in the produce for transhipment into the foreign deep-sea vessels. But during the eighteenth century monopolies and trade restrictions imposed by the Dutch created hardship in Malacca which was dependent upon foreign markets for even the common necessities of life. In 1795 it was reported[3] that any breach of the exclusive trade of the Dutch in tin, pepper, opium, spices and Japan copper was punishable by death. However the Malays, finding a ready sale for their goods in Penang were going there in *praus* despite the vigilance of the Dutch, thus contributing to the decline of Malaccan trade.

Wilting in Jakarta's Pelabuhan Kali Besar there comes the thought that it was here that so many deaths occurred among the early merchant venturers; those in the service of the Dutch East India Company and visiting seamen. The mind dwells on the past and, even though the old conditions no longer prevail, it is difficult to dispel the thought that one might yet fall victim to the 'bloody flux'. Of course precautions can be taken to minimise malarial infection and prevent other debilitating complaints. Even so the very first feeling of lassitude tends to make one think that he is about to suffer the same fate that befell many a European in old Batavia. As the Dutch Captain Stavorinus related, this was 'one of the most unwholesome spots upon the face of the globe.'

Above: *Praauwen, Eylant Rotterdam*, circa 1700. From *Oost Indien*, Francois Valentyn, courtesy Auckland Institute and Museum. Eylants Amsterdam and Rotterdam are two islets near Onrust Island where the Vereenigde Oost-Indische Compagne established a dockyard. They are situated a short distance offshore, north-west of present-day Jakarta. Here Valentyn shows a single-hulled *prau* with an outrigger connected to the main hull with a number of spars. Again the vang is absent and there is no spar at the foot of the sail.

Right: *Pelabuhan* Kali Besar, the great *prau* harbour of Jakarta's Sunda Kelapa, starts where the Cilliwung River ends at Pasar Ikan. It originated during the 17th century as two breakwaters jutting out into the sea. Subsequent reclamation has resulted in a long canal of great commercial importance.

During the mid-eighteenth century the mortality rate among the Europeans in Batavia generally fluctuated between 1,000 and 2,000 in a year and sometimes exceeded 2,000 which represented up to a quarter of the total number of arrivals at the port in a year. Ships' crews in a poor state of health because of the hardships suffered during a long voyage were particularly vulnerable to more serious disease to which even those in good health often succumbed. A visit ashore one day and the next life might already be on the wane. The odours that arose from the foul canals bespoke of death in the offing. Cook, in the *Endeavour*, was here between October and December 1770 and was powerless to prevent the loss of six of his crew before he sailed. Neither could the physician aboard the *Indefatigable* prevent a like loss among the crew and passengers during a similar period of time (Sept.–Nov.) thirty-five years later.

Despite Batavia's death-dealing atmosphere, in the 1830s a traveller[4] was able to admire the beauty of fishing *praus* with their mat sails as they sailed between the numerous offshore islets. So swift were they that a square-rigged merchantman making for the roadstead at seven knots was overtaken 'with great rapidity' by those coming in from the sea. Some of them were calculated to be of from fourteen or fifteen tons burthen, each carrying a single square sail. In the strong breeze that was blowing a plank was thrust out to windward as a balance board on which several of the crew precariously crouched.

Very early in Batavia's development as a port the Kali Besar that gave shelter to small craft was confined between two breakwaters so that the current created would scour a channel free of mud. The breakwaters now extend much further out to sea and the land on each side has been reclaimed, the area to the east forming the quay for handling today's *prau* traffic. The *praus* are still tracked along the western bank of the Kali Besar as they were a century and a half ago on the east bank.

Above: The *pinisi Nur Laila* outward bound from Sunda Kelapa. The sails have yet to be freed from their lashings and the quarter rudders lowered.

Right: Timber, flour, cement and household commodities comprise the cargoes of the *praus* in Sunda Kelapa. This must be the busiest sailing ship harbour anywhere in the world and certainly rivals old Makassar which was the home port of numerous Bugis *praus* in the past.

Left: At the seaward end of Sunda Kelapa's Kali Besar *praus* prepare for sea while others await the arduous haul to a discharge berth. Most of these craft are two-masted *pinisi* but sloops are in among them, and a strange pole-masted ketch.

Below: Ship chandlery at Pasar Ikan, Jakarta. Synthetic fibre has replaced coir in the manufacture of rope.

Above: The timber-laden *pinisi Cahaya Mutiara* is slowly hauled along the Kali Besar. In the morning this is but one of a long line of *praus* seeking a berth. In the afternoon others will be outward bound.

Above right: To avoid conflict outward bounders move out of the harbour together. Poling with long bamboos is resorted to and a line to the capstan helps.

Right: Part of a fleet of *praus* waiting to enter Sunda Kelapa, Jakarta's *prau* harbour. They are moored between the partly submerged breakwaters that run out to sea to minimise the silting up of the channel.

Left: A close look at the quarter rudder mounting of the *Nur Laila*. At sea the rudders are held in recesses in the cross-bearers. Tillers point aft. Here a spare rudder is being carried.

According to the Code

The Malays, at the time of the entry of Europeans in South East Asian trade, were probably second only to the Chinese as a maritime people—in this part of the world anyway—and their influence was, and still is, very noticeable in certain craft of the *prau* type throughout Malaysia and the Indonesian islands that extend for hundreds of miles to the south-east of Malacca Strait. For centuries there has been an ever changing pattern of trade in these waters. The Chinese came in their junks to consort with the Malays in their *perahus* (*praus*) while the Arabs and Indians made seasonal voyages in their dhows. Participating in the rich trade of this area were the Bugis seafarers from the south of Sulawesi. They were blamed for much of the piracy that took place in these waters but groups of marauders operating from outlying islands were often responsible for the illicit raids on shipping. The Sulu Sea was particularly notorious for pirates and in 1843 the survey ship *Samarang*, while off Brunei, received a report that there was a fleet of a hundred piratical *praus* lying off Balabac.

The Malays were known to have *praus* equipped for piracy long after the Portuguese had become established in Malacca even though there had been for many years a rigid Maritime Code in force to keep those connected with the sea within the bounds of the law. It is thought that this code was introduced to the Malays during the thirteenth century following the adoption of the Islamic faith by Sultan Mahmud Shah. The code was accepted, with certain amendments, by the majority of the Sulawesi states which included the home territory of the Bugis and Makassar sailors so that the original laws of those people were superseded by those of the Malays. As late as the nineteenth century this Maritime Code was being used as a basis to maintain discipline afloat and ashore and even today its tenets could be employed to some advantage.

'. . . let the law be administered at sea that no disputes and quarrels may take place – let them be known and descend to posterity, that man may not act according to their own will and inclination, but that order and regularity may prevail on board vessels, as well as during prosperity as adversity – let not what is established be done away, nor these laws be resisted or disobeyed.'

The *nakhoda* (master) administered the Maritime Code aboard a *prau*, 'for as the Raja is on shore so is the Nakhoda at sea', and any person who questioned his authority offended against the law. The Code also stated that the *kemudi* (helmsman) 'shall be as the *Bendahara*' or Prime Minister 'and the *Jurobatus* as the *Temenggong*' (Chief Peace Officer). Their tasks involved the supervision of everyone on board and 'to negotiate right and wrong within the proa.'

It might be as well at this juncture to introduce other names of the various ranks of officers and crew that were used aboard *praus* during the time of and preceding the nineteenth century and to state some of the duties of those seafarers. The *malim* was the chief officer—the *malim besar* or 'big' *malim*. The *malim kechil* or 'small' *malim* came next in rank and he could be likened to the European second mate. He was also termed the *malim angin* and his main responsibility was to handle the sails according to the requirements of the *malim besar* so that he might hold the *prau* on her correct course. In Indonesian *praus* steering was universally by the *kemudi* or quarter rudder and in

Left: Disentangling bowsprits in the Kali Besar, Sunda Kelapa.

Left: The *nakhoda* of the *pinisi Cinta Usaha* demonstrates his box of tricks.

Near right: The barber of *Komala Sari*. The Madura *leti-leti* is at Kali Baru, Jakarta.

Far right: Rice forms the basis for Rusdi Sud's mid-day meal aboard the *Budi Agung* from Ujung Pandang.

Below: Crew of the *sekoci Sumber Jaya*.

the modern vessel, even though the quarter rudder is no longer used the wheelhouse is known as the *kamar kemudi*—the steering room or cabin.

A *jurobatu*, as named in the Maritime Code, alluded to the seaman whose task it was to attend to the anchor and all the work associated with the fore part of the *prau*. A *tukang* could be likened to a petty or intermediate officer (quartermaster) and each one had a specific task to perform. The *tukang agung*, for instance, as the chief petty officer, attended to the mainmast. After him in importance was the *tukang kiri* who was responsible for work on the port side of the *prau* and then there was the *tukang kanan* equally as responsible for work on the starboard side. In charge of the hold was the *tukang petak* and the *anak* were the ordinary seamen some of whom might have been slaves or debtors.

For the maintenance of discipline it was the law that the *tukang kanan* and the *tukang kiri* should possess a respectable influence and perform their duties with the *tukang agung*. All *tukangs* worked under the direct orders of the *nakhoda* and the lesser members of the crew under the *tukangs*.

The so-called Makassar Code differed from that of the Malay in that the owner of a *prau*, instead of the *nakhoda*, took over the 'authority of a Raja' with the *nakhoda* becoming the owner's *bendahara* or 'Prime Minister'. Justice was administered by the *temenggong*, the officer responsible for peace and order, who would have been a *tukang*.

In a large *prau* the *nakhoda*'s work load was eased by the employment of a *jurotulis* whose duties were similar to those of a purser. Also on board there might be those people who had some pecuniary interest in the voyage, perhaps owning a proportion of the cargo or having some other investment to watch over. Wages were paid only to those who acted in the place of an indisposed crew member or one who was otherwise unable to take part in the voyage. Raffles, in his translation of the Code explained that even though every person on board had some commercial speculation in view it was not necessarily very great and engagements were made for one voyage only.

Monetary loans were made by the owner or the *nakhoda* of a *prau* to those partaking in a voyage or, alternatively, some shares in the cargo were allocated to them so that the voyage

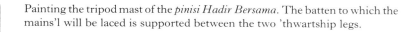

really was a commercial enterprise involving everyone on board the *prau*.

Discipline was strict and the Code laid down some heavy penalties for certain offences: such as the cutting off of a hand for theft. Such punishment might appear to have been unduly severe yet it still persists in some countries. It must also be remembered that, at the same time such a punishment was legal according to the Malay and Makassar Maritime Codes, keel hauling was a recognized form of sentence in the English men o'war and if carried out was one from which the victim might very well not survive. And in the *praus* there was no punishment to compare with being lashed to a mast and having spikes forced into the mouth—a seventeenth century punishment for swearing!

When a member of a *prau's* crew disobeyed the *tukang angung's* orders he was handed over to the *jurobatu* (the seaman responsible for the fore part of the *prau*) whose task it was to administer seven lashes to the wrongdoer. The severity of such punishment however was to some extent controlled by a clause in the Code which stipulated that 'the stripes shall not be inflicted with an uplifted or powerful arm.' If after punishment an offender continued to defy the *tukang's* orders a further four lashes could be given.

An *anak* or common seaman of a *prau* was under the immediate control of the *tukang tengah*, the officer who acted as guard, and the Code stated that 'If any person resists his authority he shall, in the manner above described, be punished in the presence of the *temenggong* with three times seven stripes and if the offender still resists the authority of the *tukang* it shall be lawful for the *temenggong* to hang him up (by the arms) and to punish him with three stripes more.' A seaman who was neglectful of his duty or disobeyed the order of a *tukang* would receive his punishment at the fore hatch, seven stripes being the usual sentence for such an offence.

Right: Preparing a meal before the fire box aboard a *pinisi*.

Below: A capstan helps to ease a *pinisi* along the Kali Besar at Sunda Kelapa. This photograph also shows the clamping together of the tripartite bowsprit.

At Ujung Pandang in Sulawesi a 'This Way Up' sign is disregarded. The modern *pinisi* with its sleek bows is a far cry from the old Bugis *prau's* form of construction.

The Maritime Code not only dealt with the discipline of the seamen but also saw to it that the senior officers were punished for what were considered serious offences. For instance should a *malim* be found guilty of losing a *prau* through neglect or carelessness he might well lose his life. The *malim's* position was one of great responsibility and the law demanded that he stay with his *prau* for the whole voyage and at no time during a voyage could he be permitted to relinquish his command. On the other hand any *juromudi* or *jurobatu* who wished to leave could do so on making certain payment.

As we have seen, sometimes there were those on board a *prau* who had some interest in the cargo that was being carried. Their presence probably contributed in no small degree to the success of the voyage. A wide range of regulations governed a crew's participation in the commercial side of a voyage and the Maritime Code not only protected participants but saw to it that each person aboard a *prau* carried out his duties in a proper and efficient manner so that at no stage would life or the safety of the *prau* be in jeopardy.

Officers and crew were allowed specific parts of the *prau* for recreation and a section was allocated for business purposes or where any important consultation could take place between senior officers. Seamen were punished if they trespassed on certain sections of the *prau* which included the part where the ropes were kept. Only the *tukangs* were allowed immediately forward of the *nakhoda's* cabin. Such regulations have a parallel in modern vessels where certain areas like the bridge and engine room are absolutely forbidden territory to unauthorised personnel, and passengers, unless invited.

The safety of a *prau* was one of the prime considerations of all aboard especially with regard to fire which could so easily occur where there was an open cooking place and so much bamboo and *atap* used in the vessel's construction. It was the responsibility of the *tukangs* to see that all precautions against fire were taken by the crew. Regulations provided that immediately after the cooking of a meal the galley fire was to be

Crew of the *Komala Sari*. The barber has donned his best shirt for the photograph.

extinguished. If any fire occurred through neglect of such action then the person responsible would be liable to receive two lashes from everyone on board the *prau*. In the event of a slave causing the fire his owner was liable to a fine and should he not be in the position to pay it the slave would receive four lashes.

Should heavy weather make it necessary to jettison cargo some agreement had to be arrived at as to what proportions of the various owners' cargo would go over the side. It was the *nakhoda's* responsibility to see that such a decision was made and the operation carried out fairly. It cannot be imagined how each owner's cargo could have been jettisoned in the proportions decided upon for some must surely be at the bottom and quite inaccessible.

In the event of a *prau* being lost through running ashore or sinking after a collision with another *prau* that loss would not be considered to have occurred by accident but through some fault that could have been avoided or by negligence. Precautions were expected to be taken that kept vessels out of such disaster. However there were provisions for compensation.

The awkward and most inconvenient positioning of the tillers in the older type of Bugis *palari* has often drawn comment from those who appreciate the discomforture the helmsmen must endure. The reason usually given is that by sitting astride a wooden bar and being compelled to steer with the feet one had no option but to remain awake otherwise he would fall overboard. Watches had a minimum duration of six hours and sleeping at the helm had to be effectively discouraged. Yet opium smoking by the crew was permitted with the Code saying 'It is the usage that the persons on watch shall each be allowed convenience for smoking opium, in order that they may not fall asleep during the time it is necessary for them to keep watch.' Can it be assumed that the pleasures of opium were regulated to off watch hours so that any drowsiness might be eliminated while actually on watch?

There was a rule that made it compulsory to hail any passing *prau* and anyone who allowed 'the people in other proas to hail first, they shall be punished with seven stripes each.' No doubt

The small *pinisi Harapan Baru* at Sunda Kelapa.

The youthful crew of the *pinisi Hadir Bersama* at Sunda Kelapa, Jakarta.

such a regulation would encourage *prau* crews to keep well beyond hailing distance and so have less chance of falling into pirates' hands. These were times when every *prau* was reckoned to be a marauder until proved otherwise.

Such mishaps as breaking away from moorings or accidental grounding were invariably judged to be caused through neglect and the *tukangs* would be reckoned as being equally as guilty as any seaman for being so stupid to allow such a mishap to occur. Twenty lashes each was considered just punishment for those actually on watch at the time. Again, in the event of a *prau* not being properly baled out then those on watch would be liable to receive fifteen lashes each. Desertion by slaves was looked upon as something to be avoided for should any defection take place through the unwatchfulness of the crew then as many as sixty lashes could be the reward. Let it be hoped that they were distributed to the whole crew!

The maintenance of good order depended so much upon the crew's observation or, according to the Code, there being a 'good lookout'. This was essential for the detection of theft. 'If the persons on watch do not keep a good lookout, and anything is stolen from the proa, they shall be punished with two stripes from every person in the proa.' This would have been quite an ordeal for the offender in a big *prau* carrying a large crew and perhaps many other people too. In the event of a slave being found guilty of theft then '. . . he shall, in the first instance, be confronted with his master; and if it appears that the master knew of the theft and did not inform the *nakhoda* or *tukang* thereof, but it reaches the *nakhoda* through other information the law is, that the slave's hand shall be cut off and the master fined as he himself had been the thief, because the law is the same with respect to the thief and the person who receives the articles that have been stolen.'

Civil law, in most respects, was the same at sea as on land but at sea the *nakhoda* of a *prau* administered justice with the crew permitted to carry out any punishment set by the Code even to the extent of putting into effect the death penalty. Adultery was a crime that carried the penalty of capital punishment and according to the Maritime Code 'If any person on board a *prau* has criminal connection with the woman of a *nakhoda* it is the law that he be put to death. If the parties are not slaves, and the woman is married, it shall be lawful for the *nakhoda* to order them both to be put to death by the crew. If the parties are not slaves and both unmarried, they shall be punished with one hundred stripes each, and afterwards obliged to marry.' Numerous other clauses covered variations of the theme as they did for fighting, where, under certain circumstances, even if the offender had not drawn his kris, it was lawful to put him to death.

Commercial law also had to be considered and it was illegal for a *nakhoda* to deviate from place to place on a voyage without agreement or some understanding with the crew for, after all, they too were involved in the voyage and any gain to be had from it was theirs also. The *nakhoda*, however, did have certain privileges and on arrival at any place he was permitted to trade for four days before any others on board should he desire to do so. Then the *tukang angan* or chief officer had the opportunity of trading for two days after which the rest of the crew would be free to join in.

Regulations governed every aspect of a trading voyage. There were such matters as duties, and tribute, to be paid to the sultans and officials in various towns or provinces where trade was carried out. Such payment was usually made with items of trade, perhaps a few bundles of rattan or maybe a quantity of gunpowder. Such things were far more useful than money which the *nakhoda* probably never had anyway!

Above: A mortar carved from a solid piece of wood is an essential culinary utensil aboard a *prau*.

Left: Rigging is in constant need of attention. Crew of a *pinisi* taking up slack in the stays.

33

Left: The *Nur Bahagia* has a single rudder lashed to the stern-post with coir while the *Bunga Melati* retains quarter rudders.

Right: A stitch in time. . . . Mending a sail on the quayside at Sunda Kelapa.

Below: The ladder arrangement erected between the two 'thwartship main-mast legs of the *pinisi Cahaya Mutiara*. The furled sail is laced to the central wooden batten. Similar ladders are also attached to the shrouds to give access to the cross-trees.

Right: The main-mast assembly of a *pinisi* with a water tank nestled between the tabernacles.

Far right: The spacious deck of a large *pinisi*, looking aft. The tripod masting is stepped in tabernacles. In the immediate left foreground is a capstan and in the center the mounting for another. Stanchions emerge from the cover-boards to give support to rails and for the securing of rigging.

Far right, below: The port rudder of the *Cahaya Mutiara*. Usually a rudder is adzed from a single baulk of timber but this one appears to be in two pieces dowelled and bound together.

Below right: The shrouds of a *pinisi* are secured to stanchions with wire.

Below: *Pinisi No. 3748LLa Bunga Melata* showing the construction of the bowsprit. Note the stowed anchors and the capstan.

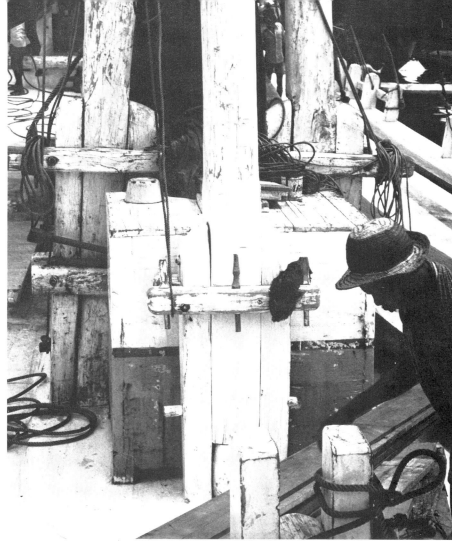

Left: The bilge pump of a *pinisi*.

Right: Looking towards the stern of *pinsi No. 3748LLa Bunga Melata*. Wooden water tanks at the foot of the mizzen mast.

Below right: A deeply laden *pinisi*, the *Cahaya London* (London Pearl) in the approach channel to Sunda Kelapa.

Below: A mast under repair at Surabaya's Tanjung Perak. Note the wooden cap and dovetailing of the cross-trees.

South Sulawesi of the Prau

In South Sulawesi the *prau* builders are of the Konjo linguistic group and separate from the Bugis who are the actual seafaring people. But in travelling along the south coast of the peninsula and turning north past Takalar, just south of Ujung Pandang, one comes into the territory of the Makassarese seafarers and then, beyond Pare Pare, into that of the Mandars. Consequently not all of the Sulawesi, or indeed the Indonesian mariners as a whole, are of Bugis extraction. Then too, old territorial barriers exist that affect not only the manning of the *praus* but also, to a certain degree, restricts the trade that they can engage in.

It is quite obvious that each area has developed its own particular type of *prau* and that they are sailed by people of the area from which they hail. It is most noticeable that in the central Java Sea the Madurese, in their lateen-sailed craft, are almost as numerous as the Bugis sailors in their *pinisi*. A visit to Kali Baru to the east of Tanjung Priok and to Semarang will prove the point.

Fifty years ago Bira in South Sulawesi was a thriving Konjo *prau*-building *kampong* with the beach lined with *atap*-roofed huts that provided shelter for craft under construction and those hauled out during the seasonal laying up period. The beach is now deserted, for no longer is there any shipbuilding industry in Bira. The *praus* are built elsewhere where timber is more easily obtained, at Tana Beru, some 15 kilometers away and at Pallengu, just south of Takalar. It is the availability of

The scintillating reflections of a *pinisi* discharging cargo at Ujung Pandang.

logs or timber that really dictates where a *prau* might be built and the cutting out of forest areas in Sulawesi has influenced the *prau* builders to migrate and establish yards closer to the timber source. Kalimantan and Sumatra now provide most of the timber for building purposes and even though it is shipped by *prau* from Kalimantan to Sulawesi many of the largest *praus* of the *pinisi* type are now constructed at Banjarmasin, Palembang or Jambi.

On Java one might be fortunate to see a *prau* being built at Gresik but the information that Rembang is a great *prau*-building centre is certainly out of date. Perhaps it was true enough when John Stavorinus, a post captain in the employ of the Netherlands States-General, made his voyage to the Indies during the years 1768–71. At that time small vessels for the Company were being built there and one of 500 tons had also been constructed. Apparently the Rembang *prau*-building industry has shifted to Sluke, approximately 25 kilometers to the north-east.

Stavorinus provides an account of *prau* building in Bira during the latter part of the eighteenth century after the territory had been ceded to the Netherlands Company through the Treaty of Bone. The country was rocky and barren although there were trees growing from which the inhabitants obtained 'middling good timber for building proas. . . . They build their proas, which they call paduakans, very tight, by dowling the planks together, as coopers do the parts that form the head of a cask, and putting the bark of a certain tree between, which swells, and then fit timbers to the planks, as at Bombay; but do not rabbet, as it is called, the planks, as is done there. In Europe we build reversely; we set up the timbers first, and fit the planks to them afterwards. They are bigotted to

old models and fixtures in fitting their vessels; the largest never exceed fifty tons; they have their bow lowered, or cut down, in a very awkward manner, so as to be often under water; a bulk head is raised a good way abaft the stem to keep off the sea. They have a tripod mast, with a high pointed sail: the tripod mast is made of three stout bamboos; two rising from the sides, and one from the fore part of the vessel, lashed together at the top: the two feet abreast are bored at the lower end across, with holes about three inches in diameter; and these holes receive the two ends of a piece of timber, which goes across, like a main shaft; on these two abreast parts of the tripod turn, as upon a hinge; the fore part of the mast is fixed forward, like a mainstay, to a knee amidships, with a forelock; by unlocking the forelock, the mast is struck in a moment.'

This description of the eighteenth century South Sulawesi *prau* could very well be applied to the present-day *prau patorani* of Ujung Pandang except that in place of the 'high pointed sail' there is an angled rectangular one or, more

Above: The Sulawesi *prau patorani* sets the old type of tilted 'square' sails on bamboo tripod masts. This is the *Turu Cinnaya* attending to offshore fish traps at Ujung Pandang.

Above right: Approaching a fishing platform off Ujung Pandang, Sulawesi. Palm fronds, bamboo and rattan feature in the construction of a *prau patorani*.

Right: The *patorani* has the old *palari* type of bow with its low fore deck and transom. The *Turu Cinnaya*.

42

generally, two, known locally as *sombala tanja* and named as *sompot* by Gibson-Hill.

It was in Sulawesi that the *prau pinisi* evolved from the *paduakan* (or *paduwakang*), a *prau* that set the traditional angled or tilted rectangular sails. But by the end of the last century the European ketch rig had been introduced to indigenous East Indies craft and this is the rig of the present-day Indonesian *pinisi* or *palari*. The transition from the original type of sail to that of the *pinisi* is illustrated in Matthes' Atlas of 1885 where a model of a *paduakan* is shown that sets tilted sails on both masts but from the main (the foremost) mast a gaff sail is also set together with two European-type jibs. The tilted squares'l or rectangular sail of the *prau patorani* differs from that of the *paduakan* only in the material from which it is made.

At Ujung Pandang in Sulawesi there is a fleet of *praus* that attend to the off-shore fish traps and which, to a lesser degree, partake in the local coastal trade. They are almost identical to the *praus* that Matthew Flinders encountered off Arnhem Land in 1803 while aboard the *Investigator* and William Westall's drawings of them portrays that similarity so well that there is no doubt as to their classification. There is the low bow and a like stern with its quarter rudder or steering oar. And set from a tripod mast is the tilted rectangular sail. I photographed *praus* similar to this off Ujung Pandang in 1978. They were built up from the low *pajala* hull (one that does not go above the strake that runs for the full length of the hull). In these *praus* though, the *prau patorani*, we find 'midship strakes that extend between the fore and after transoms, so giving those short low decks in the bows and at the stern, the latter being built over beyond the sternpost by the elongated poop or *ambeng*. This structure is most attractively proportioned and

Above: Here is the traditional double-ended Bugis *palari* hull with quarter rudders and *ambeng*.

Left: Closing in on the *Turu Cinnaya* affords the opportunity to study the construction of a *prau patorani*. The tripod masts are stepped into tabernacles.

not so cluttered with external beams, rails and stanchions as encountered in the larger *pinisi*.

The *prau patorani* is a relatively small craft about 9 meters on the water line and built very similar to the old Bugis *palari*. It possesses a gentle sheer and is usually painted white with a coloured riband along the top strake and a broader band running the full length of the hull lower down and reaching the water amidships. Little advantage has been taken of foreign contact and so this *prau* preserves much of its original character and charm. Although this means that proper cabin accommodation is lacking, shelter is provided in the shape of ridged roofing built from split bamboo and *atap* which extends from the position of the 'thwartships beam that supports the quarter rudders to amidships. Over the projecting poop an additional *atap* awning is sometimes spread providing the crew, and particularly the helmsman with a certain amount of shade.

With its tripartite bamboo masting the *prau patorani* of Sulawesi certainly has a deep association with the past. This is evident when viewing the craft portrayed in the stonework of Central Java's Boru Budur temple. Here the relationship obviously is very close despite the twelve hundred odd years that separate the carving of the image from the living *prau*. The masts are stepped in tabernacles, the foremost assembly, as the main mast, is constructed from larger bamboos than is the mizzen. The description provided by Stavorinus is equally applicable to the present-day craft but he omits any reference to the most interesting feature of the tripod mast. That is the curling over of the shaped wooden terminal block that marries the three bamboos at their head. Within it are sheaves, one above the other, for halliards. A backstay is also run aft from the centre of the curled over part of the masthead. This extraordinary fashioning is shown in early portrayals of Indonesian *praus* although usually in a somewhat exaggerated manner.

The main-mast assembly reaching, as it does, to a height of about 9 meters is in need of some climbing aid. This is provided by the two side members being bound at intervals with rattan so giving some hold for the feet of anyone going aloft.

The traditional tilted 'squares'l' is still set by the Sulawesi *prau patorani* but it is no longer made from palm matting as it was in the first place. Today a sail is made up from cotton cloths that are often printed with pastel stripes of blue or green. Strictly speaking these sails are not square. Neither are they rectangular but are of an irregular shape with both the luff and the leach concave. Some distortion is also created through the flexing of the bamboo spars between which the sails are set. Their efficiency, however, does not seem to be impaired in any way and the irregular shape has a far greater appeal aesthetically. I watched these picturesque *praus* sailing off

The *Cahaya Galesong* festooned with 'bearded' fish traps. The traditional curled-over heads of the tripod masts are clearly seen.

Ujung Pandang and such was their performance that there is every reason to believe in the saying that what looks good must be good. Even so, there is reason to doubt the usefulness of the ridiculously small sails such as are sometimes set on nothing more than a stick positioned under the mizzen-sail.

What might be considered a 'western' innovation is roller reefing but it is equally endemic to Malaysian and Indonesian waters where it is commonly employed in conjunction with the tilted sails as seen in the *prau patorani*. To furl one of these sails the lower bamboo spar—it can hardly be called a boom—is revolved by hand at its fore end so that the sail is rolled round on it until meeting up with the upper spar. The two bamboo spars and the rolled sail are then lashed together. There is no necessity to lower the upper one although this can be done as is customary in the Malay *payang* where it is gradually lowered with the rolling of the sail on to the lower bamboo spar. Through the fore end of this a crosswise peg is fitted as a grip to facilitate the winding action.

Captain Thomas Forrest, when he voyaged from the Moluccas to New Guinea (Irian Jaya) during the years 1774–76, observed numerous *corocoros* and other *praus* with the roller-reefing device. Indeed, the main-sail of the *prau* in which he made the extraordinary journey was similarly fitted. Forrest appreciated that native crewmen did not take kindly to European square sails and so, as master of the *Tartar Galley* belonging to the Honourable East India Company, he retained the large tilted squares'l and lateens, the traditional sails of the region. These continue to be used in certain types of *praus* despite the introduction of European-type gaff and jib-headed sails.

The *Tartar Galley* which Forrest had command of was a Sulu *prau* quite unlike any that are now seen in Indonesian waters. It measured twenty-five feet on the keel but because of the long overhangs at the bow and stern the overall length of the hull extended to forty feet. A peculiarity in this type of vessel was a ledge that projected about thirty inches over both gunwales on which rowers would sit when manual propulsion was required.

The main mast of the *Tartar Galley* consisted of what Forrest called 'an artillery triangle' made from three stout bamboos 'which could be struck with the greatest ease by three men'. As we have already seen such bamboo masts are commonplace today especially in the *prau patorani* of Sulawesi. In describing the sails I shall continue with Forrest's narrative[5] although to avoid the agony incurred by such passages as 'inftantly diminifhed or made fmaller by eafing or flacking the fheet' an exact transcription of the printed word is purposely not made.

On the mast 'was hoisted a large four cornered sail, called by the Malays, lyre tanjong (pointed sail), because the upper

Left: A *corocoro*, T. Forrest, *A Voyage to New Guinea and the Moluccas*.

Below: The *Tartar Galley*, T. Forrest, *A Voyage to New Guinea and the Moluccas*.

The *patorani* is an attractive *prau* even when cluttered with fish traps and bamboos.

corner appears sharp or pointed. I fixed to her a foremast close forward, and a bowsprit; and gave her a lateen, or three cornered foresail. I also gave her a lateen mizzen; but when it blew fresh, I took down the lyre tanjong from the tripod mast, as it was a very large sail, and put in its place a lateen sail. The sails then resembled those of the galley in the Mediterranean. One very great advantage attends the lyre tanjong, which is this; that when the wind freshens, it can, without lowering, be instantly diminished or made smaller by easing or slacking the sheet, and at the same time winding up the sail, by two men turning the cross bar or winch that is fixed to the inner end of the boom, and which spreads the lower part of the sail. By this means the sail may be entirely rolled up until the boom touches the yard, the sail being always in this compact manner, as seamen call it, *taken in*. In the same manner, it may be set again instantly, or let out, by turning the winch back the other way; or half set, according to the weather'.

Forrest considered that a great improvement could be made to navigation by introducing the *prau's* rig to European craft. 'Lash two London wherries together', he said, 'and give this double vessel the tripod mast and lyre tanjong, it will beat the fast sailing boats, at least three to two'.

The tripod mast and the *layar tanjong* or tilted 'square' sail have not altered much since Forrest described them over two hundred years ago and most *praus* continue to be fitted with 'two commoodies' (*kemudi* = rudder) and hulls are 'covered almost entirely with the leaves of a certain Palm tree, called Nipa'.

The *prau patorani* is often seen laden with rattan fish traps. These are similar to lobster pots and are about eighteen inches long and approximately the same diameter. At the open end long palm frond drapes are attached to resemble kelp and in this fish take shelter or search for lesser forms of life on which to feed. With this lure the more adventuresome inadvertently enter the trap to be retrieved by the *prau* crew when the pots are lifted.

All the Ujung Pandang fishing *praus* are of a similar size and rig although occasionally a single-masted one might be observed or perhaps a three-master if a diminutive stick can properly be called a mast. It appears to be the practice for these *praus* to carry two mains'ls of different size, one apparently for use in light weather and a smaller one, left rolled with its spars, ready for setting in place of the larger sail should the occasion arise. At the stemhead two short spars converge to form the

Above: Poling in shallow water off Ujung Pandang's *pasar ikan* (fish market), two fishing *praus* head out to sea.

Above right: Crew of the Ujung Pandang *prau Cahaya Galesong*.

customary side supports to a sprit which either angles forward or takes an upward curve in which case it might have some form of ornamentation at its head. I never saw a sprit put to any use apart from the placing of an end of a bamboo through a rattan loop near its top instead of using a crutch. Always at hand aboard a *prau*, these long bamboos are used for poling in shallow water, fending off in a congested *pelabuhan* or for assisting in warping to or from a berth.

There has been frequent reference to *praus* in the waters to the north of Australia as well as on the Australian mainland. This came about through Makassar fishermen making annual voyages to the Arafura Sea to gather and process trepang and it was inevitable that the *praus* would be encountered by European voyagers during their various expeditions. The boiling and curing of the sea slug was carried out ashore on the Arnhem Land coast and these operations went on unhindered, as far as is known, for about two hundred years until 1882 when the South Australian authorities, who then governed this northern territory, decided to impose licence fees and collect customs dues from the trepangers. Consequently, through the rigorous control and continual harassment, the Makassarese fishermen found little compensation for their lengthy voyages and months of labour so the industry, which largely depended on the China market, gradually diminished and finally ceased at the turn of the century.

Matthew Flinders estimated that the trepanging *praus* he saw in Arnhem Land in 1803 were of about twenty-five tons and

each carried some twenty to twenty-five men in the fleet of sixty *praus* said to be manned by a thousand. It can be seen that this does not tally with the first estimate as it averages but near seventeen hands for each *prau*. The big fleet belonged to the Rajah of Bone and communication was made with one senior trepanger named Pobassoo who had previously been on a number of voyages to Australian waters, since about 1777, and was now in command of six *praus* in the fleet.

In 1818 the Australian hydrographer Phillip King, aboard the *Mermaid*, encountered a number of trepanging *praus* off the Arnhem Land coast. The botanist, Allan Cunningham, remarked in his diary that some of these passed within fifty yards of the *Mermaid* and on the deck of each from twenty to thirty people were observed. This estimate ties in, more or less, with that of Matthew Flinders' individual one of twenty to twenty-five in each *prau*. A water colour that survives the King expedition shows the *praus* with double, or upper and lower,

tilted sails set from a tripod mast. Another illustration of *praus* with similar sails is a wash drawing by Lieut. Owen Stanley of H.M.S. *Britomart* entitled 'Macassan *praus* off Port Essington, 1840.' It appears that these double sails were a temporary innovation abandoned in favour of carrying a smaller spare sail on deck for use in case of emergency or according to the dictates of the weather.

Most of the *praus patorani* that I saw at Ujung Pandang displayed names on their transoms. The *Sinar Jaya*, *Makmur Jaya*, *Bulan Purnama*, *Turu Cinnaya*, *Harapan Jaya* and *Cahaya Galesong* were all photographed from outrigger canoes.

At Pare Pare, some 125 kilometers north of Ujung Pandang, there is a different type of fishing *prau* to that in the south of Sulawesi. It is the *sekoci*, sleek and canoe-like and in some respects similar to the Madura *prau* in hull form. Both the deep stem and stern-post come up to a point and the 'midship

The *Sama Bahagia*, a *prau* from Pare Pare in Sulawesi. The stowing of cargo above the roofing is common practice.

housing is partly of timber construction with *atap* roofing battened down with split bamboo. The low sides of the housing slope inboard but instead of the roofing coming to a ridge there is a narrow flat roof. Angled out from the base of this structure racks project to port and starboard on which the fish traps are ranged. Aft some attempt might be made to create an *ambeng* but it is little better than a framework, lacking the finish that could make it more of an integral part of the hull as in the Ujung Pandang *prau*. Steering is by quarter rudder and the cross-beam to which these are lashed also gives support to a trestle on which rest various bamboo spars when not in use. Attached to the stanchions of these trestles are loops of rattan to hold bamboo poles in a readily accessible position.

The rig of the Pare Pare *sekoci* is alien to Indonesian craft and is European in origin being that of a sloop. The mast is stepped in a tabernacle that projects through the forward end of the 'midship structure. Both the gaff and main boom are of bamboo as is the stays'l boom. In some hulls there is a tripartite bowsprit that allows a larger stays'l to be set. The gaff mains'l helps to make this *prau* recognizable as a *sekoci*. Most hulls appear to be painted a deep blue, sometimes green, above the water-line with a white top strake separated from the blue by a narrow ribbon of red or some other bright colour. It is worth noting that, as with the dhows of the Indian Ocean, there is a downward turn of the water-line at the bow and stern with an inserted segment of a colour other than that of the above-water planking and the bottom anti-fouling preparation. I am inclined to believe that this delineation of the paintwork was introduced to these waters by the Portuguese as even today similar configuration may be seen in the fishing craft of Portugal.

Although the double tilted sail seems to have become redundant I did observe another version of a double sail set by a *prau* approaching Cirebon in 1979. This *prau*, seen only at a distance, apparently was Madurese and under its oceanic lateen sail set between its twin spars was spread a rectangular sail of no mean proportions. As the vessel approached the roadstead this lower sail was taken in and then the lower spar raised and the mains'l doused by a member of the crew going aloft.

The Bugis *palari* of fifty years ago as known by author George Collins in the 1930s must now be non-existent. I certainly have seen none in the Java Sea area and it is likely that the whole of their kind was virtually wiped out during the Japanese occupation of Indonesia during World War II. Any that survived have long since gone out of commission through old age. These *praus* were low in the bows and extremely high in the stern as illustrated in William Maxwell Blake's plan of the *Bintang Satoe*, a *prau* that measured 60 feet overall, 16 feet in width and had a depth of 8 feet 6 inches. This was a good average size for this type of *prau* but the *pinisi* that has taken its place is a considerably larger craft and has a flush deck right to the stem, eliminating the low fore deck and the associated bulkhead. Later on we shall see further changes that are taking place in this type of vessel.

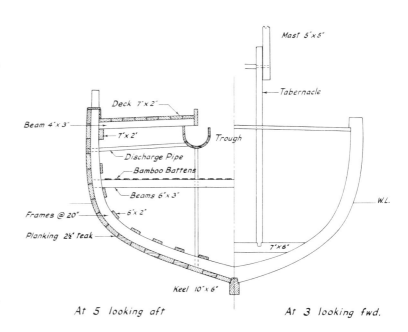

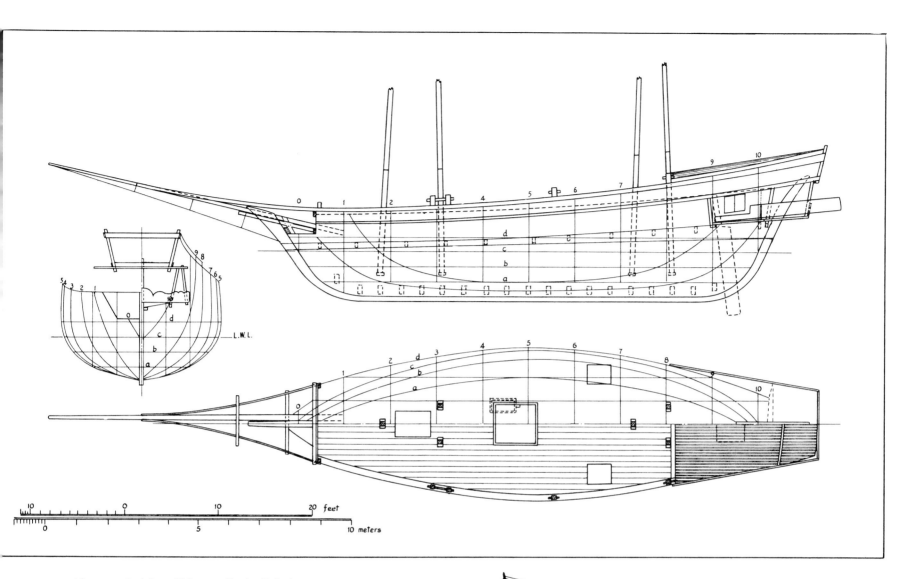

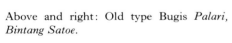

Above and right: Old type Bugis *Palari*, *Bintang Satoe*.

Left: Section through a Bugis *palari*.

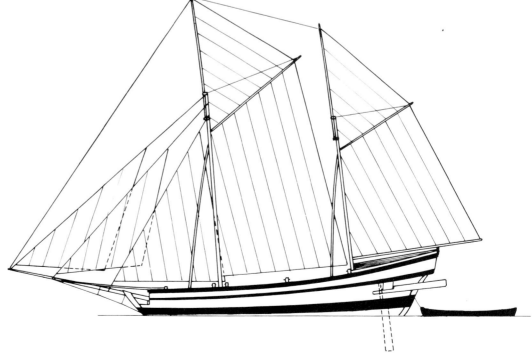

Above: Building a *prau* in Sulawesi. The curved stem and stern-post from a comparatively short keel are features of the old *palari* hull. Dowels can be seen driven into the more distant planking. (Courtesy B. Leyland.)

Left: Unruly children can make photography difficult. Here is a confrontation at Pare Pare.

Formerly each sultanate possessed its own ordinances and the eighteenth century maritime code of Bone that dealt with *prau* construction went to great lengths in stipulating specific hull measurements and advising on the acceptance and rejection of timber and the instruction of shipwrights in such matters as the necessity of positioning ribs clear of planking joints and the avoidance of knots or cracks in timber except in certain planks to be used where a hole might be considered advantageous for additional ventilation of the hull.

The old form of construction as was employed in the *palari* is still seen in the *prau patorani* of South Sulawesi although the elaborate high poop is lacking. Here, however, the hull is built according to the old traditional methods with very short planks in the bows and in the stern to take the curves and so giving a series of scarfs stepped within a short distance of each other, a circumstance that cannot but help to weaken the hull at these points.

A *palari* measuring 15 meters on the water-line would require a keel log adzed to approximately 25 cm × 15 cm. It would be slightly curved along its length with the stem and stern-post gently departing from it so that it would be difficult to determine where the keel ended and the stem and stern-posts started. At one time there was very little rake to the Bugis *prau's* stem but in the present-day *pinisi* it is considerable and in one case I measured the angle as 35 degrees from the horizontal. Planking would be finished to approximately 25 cm × 6 cm, all fastened together with hardwood dowels, slightly tapered but with a mean diameter of about 1.25 cm. Between the planks and the scarfs strips of paper bark from the *suppak* tree of Kalimantan are laid. Alternatively tarred coir is laid between planks as caulking or tar is applied only at the scarfs. Dammar resin might also be used to stop any crevices or holes.

At the *prau* building site logs are pit-sawn into planks which are then adzed with a *beliung* to their required shape and size. The holes for the dowels are drilled and with the dowels already in the previously placed plank the new one is forced into its predetermined position to be held, hopefully, for the life of the *prau*. As Stavorinus said, *praus* are not constructed like European vessels. They are planked up first and the ribs inserted afterwards. Originally the planks of a *prau's* hull were shaped with internal lugs so positioned that they corresponded with those on neighbouring planks. It was to these lugs that the ribs were lashed. The planks, of course, were dowelled together as they are today.

Prior to the introduction of European tools the construction of a *prau* must have been an extremely tedious task especially drilling the holes for the dowels. The instrument employed for this was similar to a medieval spoon gouge and in use was continuously struck with a mallet while being turned.

The *Turu Cinnaya* off Ujung Pandang, Sulawesi.

With a hull completely planked up the ribs are placed into position and fastened to the planking with treenails. These are driven home and, after drying out, given a few final blows with a mallet. A wedge is then driven into a slot in the inside face of each treenail and the ends cut off flush. So the timbers, plank and frame, are firmly locked together. The outer surface of the hull is smoothed over with an adze, a tool adequate for the task in the hands of the experienced *prau* builder. A plane is not employed for any surface work and even cabins and hatch coamings are finished off with the sharp *beliung*.

At Kali Baru to the east of Tanjung Priok I saw a plank being bent by being given the age-old fire and water treatment. This method of twisting or bending timber is employed in the absence of a steam box. One end of the plank is held down at an angle to the ground while the free end is weighted with rocks or scrap iron. Heat from a fire underneath the plank, and a frequent application of water on both surfaces with a rag wrapped round the end of a long stick, improvises for the work that a European shipwright would perform with the use of a steam box.

With a hull completed it is sealed with lime mixed with coconut oil or perhaps some substitute and then painted above the water-line and paid with an anti-fouling mixture below. It can take up to nine months for a *pinisi* to be built and rigged ready for sea but a hull could be launched within two months of laying the keel. Much depends on the energy of the shipwrights and the problems that might arise with obtaining materials or the payment for them.

Above: A *pinisi* at sea. (Courtesy B. Ives.)

Right: A sea-going *pinisi* at Sunda Kelapa, Jakarta. Here is the tripartite bowsprit at its best. The main mast is of tripod construction and the mizzen is bipod.

Far left, above: The *prau patorani Cahaya Galesong* off Ujung Pandang, Sulawesi.

Above centre: An unusual staysail in a *pinisi* at Sunda Kelapa.

Above: At Sunda Kelapa the *prau* scene changes day by day with constant arrivals and departures.

Far left: The vivid paintwork of these fishing *praus* at Cirebon reflects the artistic nature of the Indonesian people.

Left: In the Kali Besar, Sunda Kelapa, Jakarta.

Above: The *Turu Cinnaya*.

The *prau* sailor. Of the Moslem faith he usually has a friendly disposition.

Right: The *leti-leti* trails a massive quarter rudder lashed into a recess in a 'thwartship beam. There is also a recess for a starboard rudder.

Praus from Madura

William Maxwell Blake in the 1920s followed by C. A. Gibson-Hill some years later must be considered as the foremost pioneers in the study of the *praus*. The latter's brilliant work published in the *Journal of the Malayan Branch of the Royal Asiatic Society* goes a long way in laying the foundation to any further study of the Malaysian and Indonesian craft. It was indeed fortunate that during the time when both these students of maritime history were in Singapore certain Indonesian *praus*, particularly those of Madura, visited that center of Eastern trade. So it was with intense interest and certainly no small measure of delight that I first encountered the *leti-leti* at Surabaya, then at its island home of Madura and, later on, in great numbers at Semarang and Kali Baru out of Jakarta. It was with even greater surprise that I found the older *golekan* still in commission.

The Madura *leti-leti* is perhaps the most attractive of all the *praus* trading in the Java Sea. It is named, of course, after the island from which it hails, across the strait from Surabaya. It is easily identifiable with its oceanic lateen sails, double-ended hull with its beautiful sheer and the stem and stern-post rising to a high point. These deep end timbers are usually painted either blue or black above a curvilineal base line of a brighter colour. The rest of the hull is painted white apart from a coloured ribboning running along the topmost strake from stem to stern.

Closing in on Semarang the mains'l of the *leti-leti* is caught aback.

In the *leti-leti* there is a short fore deck where the cooking of meals is carried out but the greater part of the hull is covered in by a ridged roofing that angles directly inboard from the gunwales. Most of this structure consists of battened *atap* panels, the fore section of which can be raised from the bottom or slid back to permit ventilation. Alternatively the whole could be completely removed although cargo handling is usually through the forward end of the structure. A timbered cabin of greater height is situated immediately aft but with no intervening bulkhead. There is little spare room in this cabin and the main resting area for the crew is on a 'thwartship bench of woven split bamboo over the end of the hold. Aft of the cabin there is barely sufficient room for the handling of the ungainly quarter rudder and to be out of the way a water tank is hidden underneath this small decked area with access to it through a square opening in the 'midship plank of the deck.

This distinctive *prau* is certainly one that the Madurese seafarers might rightly be proud of as so much of its construction is traditional in nature and of the same kind of materials that were used centuries ago. The big main yard, for instance, is built up from a number of bamboos, neatly bound together at regular spacing to form a well balanced and beautifully tapered spar. The main boom is usually of two long lengths of bamboo lashed together to form a flexible spar upturned towards its outreaching end. The stepping of the mizzen mast, right in the stern, is at an angle of about 65 degrees from the horizontal and does not rake back but leans forward so that it rests against the cabin. The reason for this is that it eliminates the stepping of the mast in a tabernacle that would have to pass through the roofing of the 'midship structure yet allows the sail to be set in a position as far forward

as an upright mast in a more normal position would. There is also a fore lateen sail set in a most extraordinary manner from yet another forward-leaning mast. The accompanying photographs of Madura *praus* illustrate the functioning of this sail far better than would any words. In the end I saw so many of these forward-raking masts and their sails set between bamboos that they ceased to be a novelty. With regard to the rigging, the bridled main sheet is worthy of some notice as is the manner in which the mains'l is taken in by initially lifting the end of the boom.

At first I thought that there was one universal sail plan for the Madura *leti-leti* until one morning I witnessed, entering Surabaya's Kali Mas, one of these *praus* with a short upright mast stepped right in the bows and carrying a reasonably large fores'l while closer to amidships was the more expansive mains'l set from a taller mast. Within the confines of the river the mains'l was taken in and the fores'l kept drawing until the sea breeze was lost when poling had to be resorted to. In this *prau* there was no small heads'l and the rig was much like that

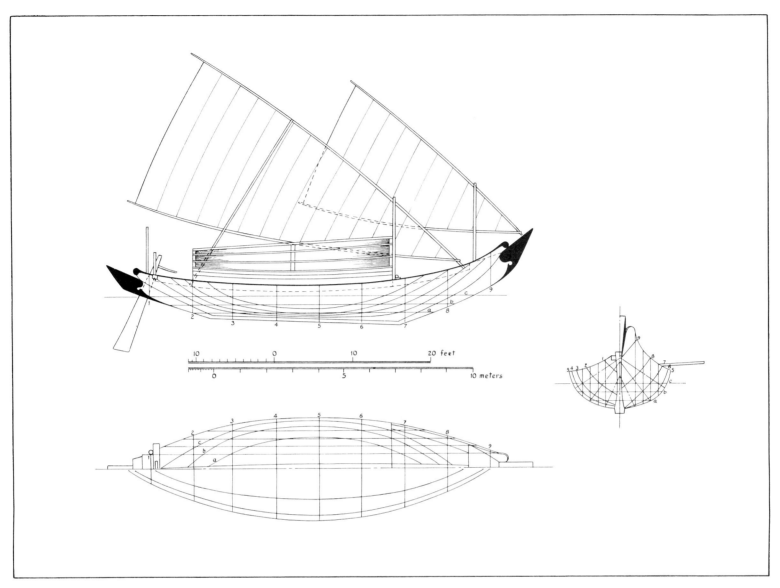

Above: Madura *prau* re-drawn from W. M. Blake.

Right: Section of a Madura type *prau* re-drawn from W. M. Blake.

Above left: A Madura *leti-leti* at sea. This *prau* lacks the cabin aft which allows the mizzen mast to be stepped further forward and consequently more upright than is usual. (Courtesy B. Ives).

Left: The *Cinta Madina*, a Madura *leti-leti* in the Kali Mas, Tanjung Perak. Illustrating the stepping of the mizzen mast, the carved crutch for the spars and the beam to support the quarter rudders.

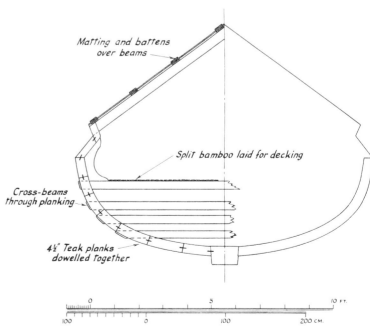

Matting and battens over beams

Split bamboo laid for decking

Cross-beams through planking

4½" Teak planks dowelled together

of a *golekan*, an earlier type of Madura *prau* that sets a fore lateen right in the bows although from a higher position than the mains'l because of the mast's stepping being at a greater height—an unusual situation but one that makes the study of these vessels so very absorbing. Perhaps this was the Indonesian version of a schooner while the more usual rig is the equivalent of the European ketch!

Besides the common Madura trading *prau* or *leti-leti* some *golekans* are still to be seen although the majority of them are of a slightly different form of construction than those photographed by Blake at Singapore during the 1920s. I was fearful of photographing those at Semarang as territorial guards were all too ready to use their rifles and I had just previously experienced one confrontation and been prevented from using my camera aboard a timber-laden *pinisi*. Blake's photographs show a projecting 'V' faced stem with a wide curling over of the meeting gunwales immediately abaft of it, and a similar formation in the stern. The *golekans* at Jakarta's Kali Baru, however, possessed a wider 'V' transom of vertical timbering with the hull planking taking off directly from it. Instead of the face of a transom being a single panel with its associated foliated artistry (as in Blake's photographs) these *golekans'* transoms were divided into panels, each decorated individually but with matching designs incised into the wood and painted predominantly in blues and chromes. In one transom the upper panel on each side of the sprit bore armorial symbols,

Above: The mains'l is furled by the lifting of the bamboo boom. It is then neatly stowed between the boom and the yard. The main yard is built up from a number of bamboos bound together with rattan.

Right: The *golekan Priama Babu* at Kali Baru, Jakarta. Typical of these *praus'* construction are the beams projecting through the hull planking and the wooden 'pick' anchors, stockless and with a weighted shank.

Far right, above: The Madura *leti-leti*.

Far right, below: A feature of the *golekan* is the tremendous sheer in the bows. (W. M. Blake. Courtesy Science Museum, London.)

obviously of Netherlands origin. Painted panels also appeared on the main hull planking at the bows. But what thrilled me most of all was the bifid construction of these *praus* with their monstrous upreaching projections breaking water at both bow and stern.

I first came across bifid construction in the Madura coasting *praus* sailing in and out of the Kali Mas, the Golden River of Tanjung Perak at Surabaya and later in the small fishing canoes on Madura Island but the bifid *praus* at Kali Baru were ocean-going *golekans* of something like 15 meters on the waterline. The bow projection of these *praus* resembles the ram of an ancient European war vessel or, if you like, the forefoot projections of certain modern freighters which it preceded by many untold centuries. However, whereas the purpose of the scientifically designed appendage is known, that of the *prau's* crude projection, from both ends of the hull, is only conjectural.

In retrospect let us see what has already been said about bifid construction. First of all I refer to James Hornell[6] whose reasoning is probably better than any other offered, coming as it does from a researcher who has contributed so much to maritime history. He considered that the extraordinary form of construction appeared to be due to the fact that the early boatbuilders concerned had not learned to curve up the ends of the keel into a stem and stern-post so terminated it in a long ram-like manner in a projection beyond the hull at each end.

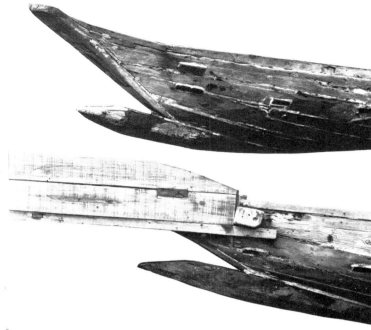

However, the indications are that in Indonesia the *prau* builders did curve up the stem and stern-post from the keel from the very beginning and it is likely that the projecting keels, as in some *golekans*, developed at the same time and alongside the curved extremeties as seen in the *leti-leti* and more notably in the *palari*.

It must be pointed out that in the Indonesian *praus* the projecting keel does curve upwards, very much so in the *golekan*, and there seems to be no reason why it could not have been extended further to form a stem and, at the other end, a stern-post as shown in the accompanying diagram.

According to another authority (W. Müller, 1912) the bifid stem projection serves to fend a canoe off any reef that may be run foul of but no reason is given for having a similar projection at the stern. Perhaps it may be surmised that originally the canoe did not actually go about, when changing from one tack to another, and some still do not, and the bow alternately became the stern and *vice versa* so making it necessary for both ends to be bifid. But Müller goes on to say that the appendages were useful as a grip for hauling a *prau* ashore. The size of the Madura *golekans*, however, makes nonsense of such reasoning and in the hauling ashore of a smaller *prau* the most practical thing to do would be to skid it over poles in which case the manhandling would be done from the sides.

As good an explanation as any for having the projections, even though they might be but half submerged most of the time, is that they could help the *prau* to maintain a more true course especially when sailing close to the wind. In other words the projections would perform a similar function to that of a leeboard or centreboard. However, when it is realized that

Above left: A trading *prau* with bifid stem and stern sailing out of Surabaya's Kali Mas.

Above: The bifid bow of a Madura Island canoe. Ends of 'thwartship timbers penetrate the hull planking. Similar cross members are seen in the recently added *ambeng*.

Right: Decorative paintwork extends along the hull planking of this *golekan* but the ends of treenails, marking the location of frames, are distracting.

Below: The projecting keel of a *golekan* illustrating how it could be extended to form a stem and sternpost and so dispense with the transoms.

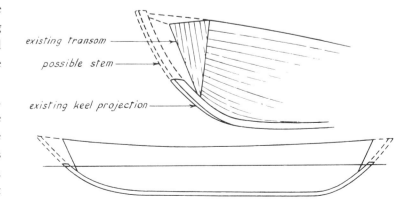

existing transom ─────
possible stem ─────
existing keel projection ─────

Left: A *leti-leti* at Tanjung Perak. Here poles are stowed on top of the roofing.

Below: The stem-head of a *Golekan* has floral decoration. The projecting ends of beams are clearly seen. A boom extends over both sides of the hull to which guys are taken from the yards. (W. M. Blake. Courtesy Science Museum, London.)

variations of the bifid construction, particularly in the bows, occur elsewhere even this theory does not hold too much water. To stretch the point the original type of *palari* hull might also be considered as being a form of bifid construction. Possibly the low bow and stern with the associated transoms came about as a development of the bifid hull ends to which the seafarers of these waters had become accustomed long before any European influence on any Indonesian *prau* occurred.

In recent times the *palari's* traditional low bow skimming the surface of the sea gradually became higher until now, in the *pinisi*, the fore transom has been dispensed with and the main deck is flush right to the stem. In some *pinisi* of recent build the bows might even be likened to those of an American clipper ship although the tripartite bowsprit mars such a comparison. In Indonesia the only explanation for the bifid stem and stern is that it is traditional.

Continuing the description of the *golekan*, one of the most important features is the projection of the 'thwartship beams on the outside of the hull. In doing so they give added strength to the hull by locking the two sides together. The beam ends are very clearly shown in the Blake photographs of 1928 some of which were used to illustrate the Admiralty publication of 1944. Unfortunately two of the *golekans* are named as being the *Siantieroo Djaja* (figures 33 & 34) and it is impossible to identify which photograph is actually of that *prau*. For this reason I prefer to leave both unnamed.

The excessive flare or overhang of the sides of the *golekan's* hull is a feature that contributes to the making of a very tender vessel. In fact, according to the marine historian James Hornell, the very name *golekan* refers to crankiness and maybe that is the reason why this vessel has gone out of favour. But what a magnificent sheer those *praus* of Blake's time had with

Right: Leaving Singapore, a *golekan* spreads its oceanic lateen sails between flexing bamboo spars. The main yard is given additional support with a bamboo prop and bamboos are also used to clear the sails from the fore ends of the yards—an extraordinary arrangement. (W. M. Blake. Courtesy Science Museum, London.)

Below: The Madura *leti-leti*.

the gunwales sweeping up to a great height in the bows and terminating in an architecturally perfect reversed curve which was repeated in the stern.

The masts of a *golekan* are extremely short stumps. One is stepped right in the bows and the other about five meters further aft and hard against the facia of the 'midship roofing. The spars which they support are of such a size that it is difficult to believe that they are actually bamboos for often their diameter at the base might be in the vicinity of 13 cm. These are suspended so close to their fore or lower end that the upper part of the spar carrying the big mains'l requires support from a bamboo pole run out from the leeward side of the deck immediately aft of the 'midship roofing. Guys for steadying bamboo yards run out to the end of an outrigger that projects about three meters over the windward gunwale just forward of the roofing. It is not unusual for this outrigger to have an upward curve so making it less likely to be immersed and possibly carried away in a heavy sea. It also appears that in some of these *praus* the outrigger can be shifted from one side to the other according to the tack the *prau* is on but in some instances the outrigger reaches out on both sides of the hull.

Apart from its construction and rig the *golekan* is readily identifiable by the painting of the hull in hues of brown and chrome, more especially in the upper planking. It was the outstanding colour scheme that initially drew my attention to a *golekan* at Semarang as all the other Madura *praus* that surrounded it were painted predominantly white.

Right: The *leti-leti* sets the oceanic lateen sail.

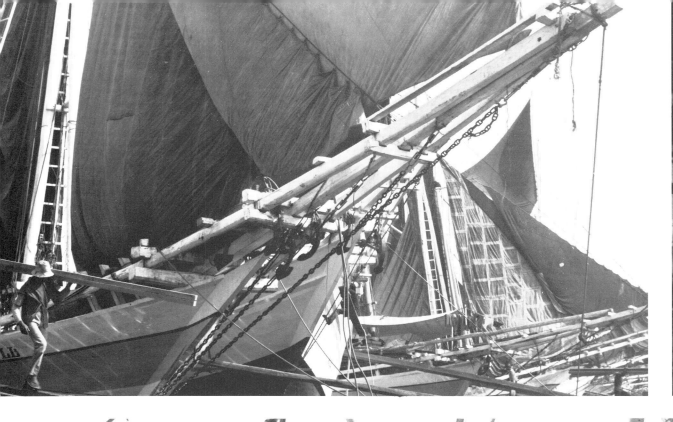

Far left: At Sunda Kelapa, looking north. In the foreground is the *Bunga Melati*.

Left: the crew's quarters of a *golekan*. Weapons are readily available for use in case of any attack. (W. M. Blake. Courtesy Science Museum, London.)

Below left: A survivor from another age. The *golekan* with its beautifully decorated transom bow and peculiar 'bifid' keel extension. The stern is of similar construction and decor.

Below: At Sunda Kelapa *praus* spread their sails to dry after overnight rain. Looking south.

A *golekan* from Madura. (W. M. Blake. Courtesy Science Museum, London.)

Above: In the hold of the *golekan Priama Babu*. Looking aft the rounded form of the hull is shown in the framing.

Above: The purpose of the *golekan's* outrigger spar is clearly seen from ahead. (W. M. Blake photograph. Courtesy Science Museum, London.)

Below: Carving at the end of a *golekan's* bowsprit.

76

Left: The wooden anchor of this *golekan* is weighted with scrap iron. In this *prau* there is also a carved 'cathead'.

Right: In this transom bow of a *golekan* the top panels show some influence from the Netherlands.

Below: Looking forward in the *Priama Babu*. Again the flare and the wide arc of the bilge can be seen.

Aloft and Alow

Prau construction certainly is varied. Some hulls have a pronounced sheer while others lack it. A stem might be perfectly upright yet another angled in the extreme. There are also differences in sterns with some as sharp as the bow and others with squared transoms. Indeed, in the old *palari* and some *pinisi* you will find two transoms above a sharp-ended stern. One of them is actually built into the main body of the hull and the other more prominent one is at the end of the cantilevered poop. Then, by way of a change, quarter rudders are sometimes dispensed with in favour of a more conventional one either on pintles or lashed to an extremely angled stern-post by way of perforations.

The long overhanging poop structure or *ambeng* is seen in diverse forms in several types of *prau* and even in some small *koleks*. In the *pinisi* it is more an integral part of the hull than it is in the Sumatran sloop or *nadé*. The latter is specifically named because this type of *prau* also comes from other islands in Indonesia. Its hull is very much like that of the two-masted *pinisi* but there are sometimes variations which are described later on. The shape of the *pinisi* is often reproduced in models made by crew members aboard the *praus*. Although their workmanship is somewhat crude the main features are accurate and these include the rigging.

At Tunjung Perak I took some measurements of a big *pinisi* named *Sinar Kumala* having an overal length of 28 meters and a beam of 8.5 meters. It is not customary for these *praus* to have draught marks engraved but, with a clean hold, it was possible to measure the depth between under deck and floor as 2.5 meters. Making allowances for the frame, keel, beams, etc., it can be assumed that this *pinisi*, laden with some 200 tonnes of cargo, would have a draught of approximately 2.75 meters. The unladen freeboard, taken amidships, was 1.8 meters. The assumed laden draught appears to be reasonably correct and compares favourably with the measurement of 7 feet (2.13 meters) given for a fifty-foot (15.24 meters) *palari* by Gibson-Hill. Also, in the plan of the fifty-foot *Bintang Satoe*, with a beam of 17 feet (5.18 meters), the draught scales to 7 feet (2.13 meters).

The *pinisi*, like the *palari*, is steered with twin quarter rudders although sometimes you will see one of these vessels with a single rudder hung from a slanting stern-post and either on pintles or lashed through apertures. Where quarter rudders in a *pinisi* are concerned heavy beams pass completely through the hull, one above the other, or almost, and in the ends of these, semicircular recesses are cut facing aft in which the rudders are securely lashed. The rudders are always withdrawn from the water while a *prau* is in harbour to prevent them from being damaged through fouling. The framework associated with the poop structure and the housing of the rudders appears, at first sight, unnecessarily complicated but every beam, stringer and stanchion serves a purpose, even a swinging spar that can be lashed in to a stringer and thereby enable the helmsman to have greater control over the rudder because of the spar's locking effect on it.

This bow view of a Sumatran *nadé* accentuates the flare of the hull and shows to advantage the construction of a tripartite bowsprit.

The *prau pinisi*

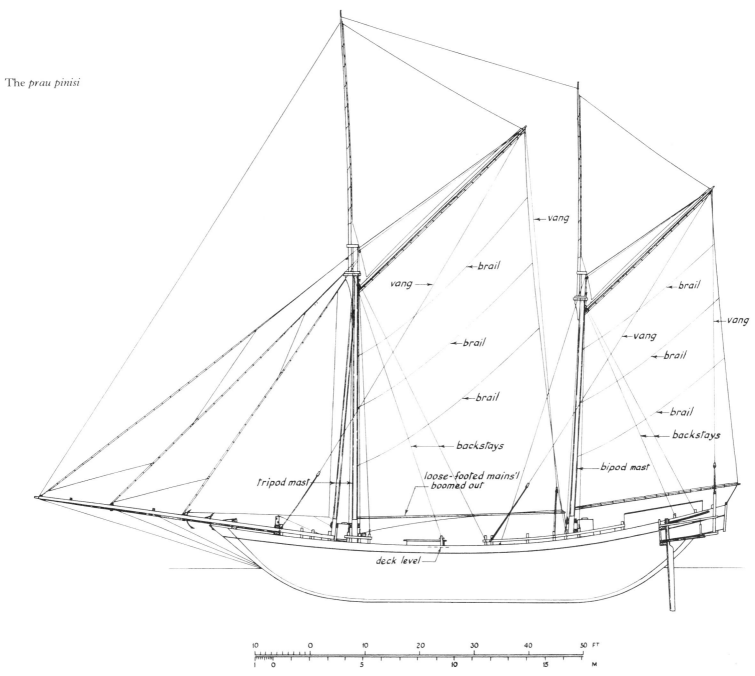

vang

brail

vang

vang

brail

brail

brail

brail

brail

backstays

backstays

tripod mast

loose-footed mains'l
boomed out

bipod mast

deck level

10	0	10	20	30	40	50 FT

1	0	5	10	15	M

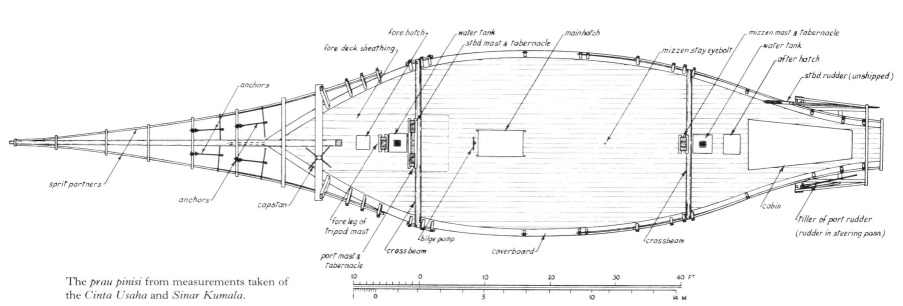

fore hatch

water tank

mainhatch

mizzen mast & tabernacle

fore deck sheathing

stbd mast & tabernacle

mizzen stay eyebolt

water tank

after hatch

stbd. rudder (unshipped)

anchors

sprit partners

anchors

capstan

fore leg of
tripod mast

port mast &
tabernacle

bilge pump

cross beam

coverboard

crossbeam

cabin

tiller of port rudder
(rudder in steering posn.)

The *prau pinisi* from measurements taken of
the *Cinta Usaha* and *Sinar Kumala*.

10	0	10	20	30	40 FT

1	0	5	10	14 M

Some *praus*, like this one at Jakarta, are built without the traditional quarter rudders.

Below: The *palari* rudder.

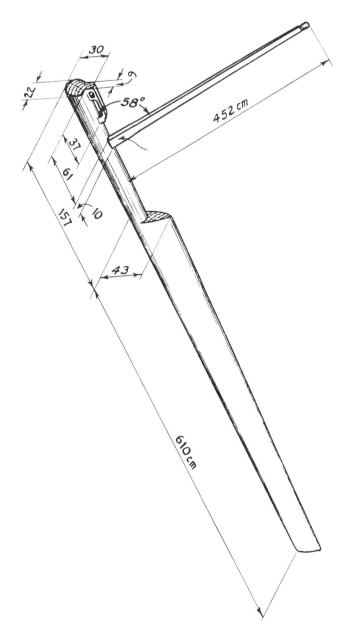

Originally a *palari*, the forerunner of the *pinisi*, had its tillers pointing outwards and the helmsmen had to sit astride the outboard *ambeng* framework and steer with their feet. In the large *pinisi* of more recent build, however, it points almost directly aft, in a slightly inboard direction, so that, although the helmsman still steers from within the framework, he does not have to overstretch himself when putting the helm over.

The rudders are extremely long and narrow blades and in the big *pinisi* the combined length of post and blade adzed from a single baulk or log measures at least six meters. A rudder in the *pinisi Cinta Usaha* was measured and the blade was 15 feet × 18 inches and the post 8½ inches in diameter. This post measurement continued for some distance close to the fore edge of the blade but gradually diminished towards the foot. At the head of the aft side of the post and fashioned out of the same baulk of timber was a lug through which a lashing could pass. Also, two strong pegs in the upper rudder support beam helped to keep lashings from slipping. The tiller was inserted in a slot about two feet from the head of the rudder post and curved gently upwards to be at a position convenient for the helmsman.

I was much intrigued by the suspension of these rudders, so much so that I made a small scale model of one from a piece of teak just to prove that they do actually float at a level that allows them to be lashed so conveniently to the cross beams. Sure enough the miniature blade sank in the water exactly to the depth corresponding to full scale. In operation a rudder is weightless so that the lashings are quite adequate for holding it in position for steering purposes. Should conditions warrant it both port and starboard rudders are manned, otherwise the use of the leeward unit is preferable because of its deeper

81

Above: The quarter rudders of a *pinisi* are withdrawn from the water while in port. The *Cahaya Mutiara* is a modern *prau* of the *pinisi* type and has a transom stern which gives the projecting *ambeng* greater width.

Left: Like an old scow, the beamy *Tenaga Baru* belongs to Dumai in Sumatra. The overhanging poop, or *ambeng*, is extraordinarily commodious although far from being luxurious.

Right: A *nadé* up for repair. Erected out over the stern is the *ambeng*. The rudder post will pass beyond the decking and the tiller in through the opening where the youth poses for the taking of his photograph.

immersion. Light weather observations, however, indicate that either rudder may be used and sometimes, when running free, there is no helmsman at all at the tiller. It is obviously the manner in which the rudder is secured to the cross beams that permits the helm to be left unattended. The rope, and occasionally rattan, lashings are made taut with a short bar used as a Spanish windlass as if applying a tourniquet.

It is of some significance that when making an ocean voyage a boxed compass mounted in the steering platform may be used. This is shown in the original plan of the Bugis *prau Bintang Satoe* as drawn by Blake some time before 1930. This plan is particularly valuable in that it is of an older *palari*, high in the stern and low forward. Here is the original tripartite bowsprit with the main spar placed off-centre to avoid the stem-head and the side members taking off from the hull at main deck level. In the modern *pinisi* all three spars of the tripartite sprit take off above the deck, the outer members being slightly higher than the main spar at their take off from the hull making it possible for the cross pieces to pass between them.

The similarities and differences of hull form in the various *praus* could be the basis for some serious study. In some examples the relationship is clear but in others there is none

whatsoever. The hull of the Madura *leti-leti* differs from that of the *golekan*. The Sumatran sloop or *nadé* possesses a flare for the full length of its hull the like of which is rarely seen elsewhere yet the *nadé* from Sulawesi has a hull more in keeping with that of a *pinisi*. Most of the two-masted *pinisi* do have something in common though and that is the manner in which they bulge to such an extreme breadth amidships, a peculiarity that provides a most expansive deck area. This is made even more capacious through the small hatch being placed well forward. Some of the sloops, however, often have a long hatch, practically the width of the deck, built up as if it were a cabin and with an opening at each end through which the cargo is handled. Wooden water tanks are usually positioned between the masting or adjacent to it and the open firebox for cooking purposes is placed wherever it might be convenient, even on top of a deckload of timber.

While in port the *pinisi* deck is sheltered by an awning and, with table and chairs knocked up on board, the crew and any visitors may find relaxation or conduct business in reasonable comfort. In the big *pinisi Cinta Usaha* of Jakarta I found that accommodation was provided in a properly constructed cabin right aft with the *nakhoda's* quarters in its forward end. So low is the ceiling height in these cabins that it is impossible to stand

Below left: Deck arrangement and rig is shown to advantage in this photograph of a *nadé*. There is a long hatch to aid the stowing of mangrove poles. The gunter rig is interesting but not new in Singaporean waters.

Right: The *prau's* galley is out on the open deck and meals are cooked in a fire-box that can be positioned wherever it might be convenient, even on top of a timber cargo.

Below: Some Indonesian *prau's* continue to visit Singapore. The *Cahaya Bunga* of Tanjung Pinang berthed in the Kallang Estuary to discharge charcoal.

upright. Aboard the *Sinar Kumala* at Tanjung Priok I measured the cabin height as a mere 3 feet 6 inches and on the *nadé Kota Baru*, in Singapore's Kallang Basin, I squatted down in an equally confined space to watch the crew gamble at a game of dominoes. But this was far superior to any accommodation found on board some of the lesser types of *praus*. Even so, everything there was ship-shape although not exactly Bristol fashion.

In a *pinisi* the cabin often occupies practically the whole width of the narrowing poop leaving barely sufficient room for any movement aft. The steepness of the deck can also make it most difficult for anyone to remain in an upright position especially if bare footed and the deck is wet. It might be considered impolite to keep shoes on when boarding a *prau* and, not wishing to offend, I at first respected Moslem custom and left my shoes at the head of the gangplank. It was most disconcerting though to observe that spitting on the deck was indulged in without restraint. Later I kept my shoes on and found that no one was offended and I felt much better about my feet.

Masts in Indonesian *praus* are traditionally tripartite and it is known that they date back to the 8th or 9th centuries by their portrayal in the carved stonework of the Boru Budur temple in Java. The bamboo tripod masting of certain present-day *praus*, especially in Sulawesi, closely resembles that shown in the ancient masonry. I had often thought that those peculiar curled-over mastheads were purely for ornamentation but that was not so and they continue to serve a threefold purpose which those early craftsmen were unable to reproduce in stone even when grossly exaggerating the size of the mastheads. Today these are made from a single piece of wood shaped as a union to hold the three legs of a mast together at the head. In it a slot is cut to take a sheave for the yard's halliard and at the end of the curled-over part there is a hole through which a single backstay is looped.

Prau masting, whether tripod, bipod or single, is generally set up in tabernacles but there are exceptions. The tabernacles consist of posts stepped within the hull. The 'thwartship ones are angled slightly inboard to allow the port and starboard mast legs to meet aloft and so form the tripod structure with the fore leg. The masts themselves do not pass through the deck but rest on blocks within the tabernacles. Either wooden dowels or iron bolts secure the mast legs in position while 'thwartship wooden clamps at about chest height serve as pin rails. To unship a mast these clamps must first be removed by withdrawing all the bolts and dowels. As may be imagined the

Left: In busy Sunda Kelapa, Jakarta's *prau* harbour. A big *nadé* from Sumatra.

Right: An Indonesian belaying pin.

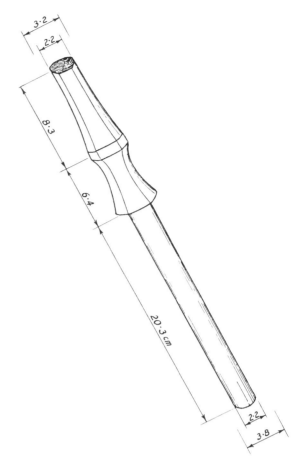

Below: Two examples of the *sekoci* at Kali Baru, Jakarta.

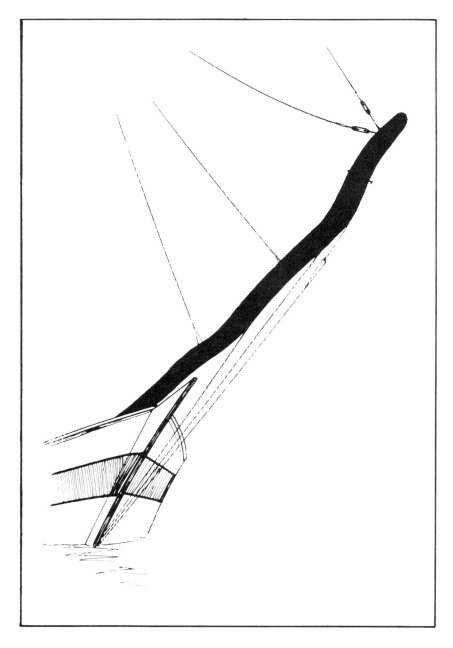

tripod mast is an extremely rigid structure so that the sub-standard rigging is of little concern.

In the plan of the *palari Bintang Satoe* the fore leg of both tripartite masts are shown bowed. Such curvature does not occur in the masting of the big *pinisi* type of *prau* now in commission and it appears to have been phased out as part of the change that is continually taking place. In this respect the tripod mast itself might very well be ousted by the bipod and single masts that are now appearing in the new *praus*. Bipod and single masts are now common in the mizzen position where a stay takes the place of the fore leg. This is secured to an eyebolt in the deck approximately a quarter of the distance from the mizzen to the main mast.

There are no chain-plates for the securing of rigging in any of the *praus* and in the *pinisi* the shrouds and backstays are looped around stanchions—actually the projecting rib ends—and under a low rail. These rails run aft from the side members of the tripartite bowsprit to the main shrouds and

Above: A shipwright's nightmare! A misshapen log has provided the main spar for this amazing tripartite bowsprit. Side supports and cross-members partially hide the malformation.

Above, left: The main bowsprit spar as it would appear without its partners. A tracing from the photograph.

Right: An Indonesian sloop or *nadé* off Singapore. (Courtesy D. Brigham.)

then there is a break to the mizzen shrouds from where the railing continues to proceed aft.

The standing rigging of many of the *praus* is very poor and set up in a most unseamanlike manner. Rigging screws are of crude manufacture and any kind of wire suffices for shrouds and stays, looped here and held by an odd shackle there, and no one seems to be at all concerned. You will also see some very deformed masts and spars but despite these failings the *praus* apparently stand up to some pretty heavy going and casualties are comparatively few.

To allow the crew to go aloft battens are seized to the shrouds and to these wooden treads are attached, in some instances by dove-tailing. Painted white, the ladders (they can hardly be called ratlines) certainly help to make the *pinisi* the distinctive craft she is. Sometimes this access to the cross-trees is provided on one side only but this would not be because of any tardiness on the rigger's part as the practice is not unknown in European craft.

As in the Singapore *tonkang* with its standing gaffs (but no topmasts) the main and mizzen sails of the *pinisi* are brailed in to their respective masts when furled. Where the masts are of tripod or bipod construction the sails are laced to a vertical batten that runs up in between the port and starboard legs of the masting. The gaff topsails are set and furled in much the same manner as those of fore-and-aft vessels in other parts of the world although they are usually laced to the topmasts instead of being seized to hoops. There is a tendency for new *praus* to dispense with gaff sails and set leg o'mutton or jib-

Above: The sloop-rigged *sekoci* is a mixture of European and Indonesian design. The long bamboo is a boom for the stays'l.

Right: The Sulawesi *prau patorani Cahaya Calesong* (Light of Calesong). The name comes from the Indonesian word for light or glow and the name of a coastal village south of Ujung Pandang.

headed sails. In such cases the main topmast is stepped between the two side legs and additionally supported by the head of the fore leg. The lower part of the luff of the mains'l is seized to the usual batten set up between the two side legs of the tripod mast but the upper part of the luff is laced to the built-in topmast. The brails are retained for drawing both main and mizzen sails in to their respective masts. The mizzen is more often than not a single pole these days with the sail laced directly to it or to a wire runner.

Left: *Kontings* at Rembang, Java.

Far left, below: The *nadé Kota Baru* in the Kallang Estuary, Singapore.

Near left, below: Bending a plank over a fire. The youth is applying a wet rag to both sides of the plank which is weighted at its free end.

Right: Floating mangrove poles ashore from a *golekan*. Kali Baru, Jakarta.

Below: A colourful cargo. Plastic containers are now replacing the old earthenware ones.

The loose-footed mains'l of a gaff-rigged *pinisi* must be jumped over the forestay of the mizzen mast when going about and when the *prau* is running free this sail's clew is held out with a spar as a spreader spinnaker fashion. There is no problem with the mizzen where it is already clewed to a boom. The peak of a gaff sail is hauled out on a runner under the gaff and the gaff topsails are set more or less according to western practice and are brought in to the doublings when furled. Sail cloth varies from light weight canvas dyed black, dark blue or brown to cotton, perhaps printed with stripes running through it, more especially in the topsails, where synthetic material is not unknown.

A large *pinisi* would carry approximately 5,852 square feet of sail made up as follows:

    Main sail 1,940 square feet
    Mizzen sail 1,235 square feet
    Main tops'l 518 square feet
    Mizzen tops'l 460 square feet
    Stays'l 754 square feet
    Inner jib 535 square feet
    Outer jib 410 square feet

For comparison the *palari Bintang Satoe* set $1,925\frac{1}{2}$ square feet:

    Main sail 610 square feet
    Mizzen sail 414 square feet
    Main tops'l 174 square feet
    Mizzen tops'l 154 square feet
    Stays'l 255 square feet
    Inner jib 150 square feet
    Outer jib $170\frac{1}{2}$ square feet

Left: The *Sekoci Macmur Jaya* at Pare Pare, Sulawesi.

Below left: The *prau sekoci*. In Tanjung Perak's Kali Mas are the sloop-rigged *Kinibalu Jaya* and *Bungamas*.

Below right: An Indonesian sloop arriving at Singapore with a load of poles. (Courtesy D. Brigham.)

On first sighting a crowded *prau* harbour one immediately becomes conscious of the fact that among the more easily recognized craft there are some strangers that at first appear to be beyond classification. Their design may not be entirely Indonesian and the rig is certainly of foreign origin. In Surabaya's Kali Mas I saw several such craft that, at the time, I was unable to identify. Later on, at Kali Baru near Tanjung Priok, similar *praus* were encountered and it was then clear to me that these were members of the *sekoci* family. That the Dutch had left their mark on them was quite obvious and for that reason it can be said that they exemplified Netherlands-colonial naval architecture. Indeed, Gibson-Hill pointed out that the word *sekochi* (*sekoci*) was derived from the Dutch *schuitje*. Today it is usually applied to *praus* that have a double-ended hull and are fore-and-aft rigged. Here then were the main clues for identifying the *sekoci* and not being confused with the *leti-leti* which sets lateen sails and therefore lacks the tripartite bowsprit.

Both the *sekoci* and the *leti-leti* have similar 'midship housing so that with the knowledge of the difference in rig it was eventually possible for me to identify one *prau* from another with no trouble at all. It is also worth noting that the *sekoci* has a rather box-like *ambeng* which is absent from the *leti-leti*.

Above: The sloop-rigged *sekoci Raja Baru* at Tanjung Perak. The hull reflects a certain element of Dutch influence in this type of *prau*. It sets a gaff mains'l and a large heads'l is taken to the end of a tripartite bowsprit.

Perhaps for aesthetic reasons the more indigenous Madura trading *prau*, with its peaked split bamboo and *atap* roofing is to be admired more than the non-descript *sekoci*. It was noticed, though, that the timbered housing of the latter *prau* was regularly doused with buckets of sea water in an attempt to keep the inside temperature down. There is no escape from the stifling 34 degrees no matter what the cabin's construction might be.

Above: Another fishing *prau* at Pare Pare. The bowsprit of the *Makmur Jaya* is to the right.

A Colourful Coast

In Bali tourists on the beaches of Sanur and Kuta become familiar with nothing more than the outrigger *praus* that cater for the demands of pleasure seeking holiday makers. Although such craft are a relatively recent innovation they do perpetuate the characteristics of the earlier sailing canoes. It is elsewhere in Indonesia that the less refined workaday canoes, the *koleks*, are to be encountered. On the canals, in remote creeks, beached within reach of the open sea or toiling within the confines of a stagnant harbour; here are *koleks* of infinite variety—dugouts, single outriggers and double outriggers, most of them for fishing. But occasionally there will be those carrying passengers, perhaps bound for the market and burdened with produce or men with their prize fighting cocks in rattan baskets bound for a battle of the spurs.

It is not intended to describe each and every canoe. There are so many of them that one might be ridden with malaria long before completing the survey but I have seen numbers enough of these craft to assure the compiler of one Indonesian-English dictionary that the *kolek* is far more than a 'small dinghy'. Some of them might be entirely dugout but others are wholly planked and, with the outriggers, the method of attachment of the floats to the booms varies according to locality. Spritsails are most frequently used in the canoes and to a lesser degree the lateen set between bamboo spars. As in the larger *praus*, quarter rudders are universally employed for steering.

At Jakarta, and in Sulawesi, there are double canoes that support expansive platforms. The canoes are connected with transversal poles upon which the bamboo structure is built. A mast is stepped in the bows of each canoe so that the lateen sails are abreast of one another. Spars reach out from the canoes and to these the masts are stayed. In the photograph of one of the Sulawesi double canoes on page 108 the sails are seen doubled up with their lower spar lifted. This is the normal way to commence the furling of one of these sails and is again illustrated in the photograph of a Madura *prau* approaching the port of Semarang (p. 64).

The platform canoes at Jakarta are much larger than those of Sulawesi and are connected with heavy timber beams or dually with bamboo and timber. In these craft, employed in fishing, there is a single mast stepped in a central position within the maze of the bamboos that form the platform.

In a creek near Pare Pare on Sulawesi I saw yet another type of platform craft. This consisted of but a single canoe with double outriggers. The bamboo platform structure was built up between these and straddled the canoe. One never knows what might be discovered hidden under the trees on the banks of Indonesia's backwaters.

In Madura there are fishing canoes that have bifid bows and sterns. Above the keel projections are 'V' shaped transoms; miniatures of those seen in the older *golekans* of this island. These canoes also have that extension, the *ambeng*, built out from the hull. Here, though, it is too small to be termed a poop but is useful enough for the fisherman's gear.

Fishermen busy aboard their *praus*. Notice the construction of the stern piece in the nearest hull and the curved arm at the head of the rudder.

99

An outrigger canoe of exceptionally interesting construction is the *jukung* of Rembang and the coast to the east of Semarang. Its hull is rather slab sided but this is because the planking is put together in the traditional manner by dowelling so making it difficult to achieve sweet lines. Consequently there is a definite shoulder where the planking changes direction towards both the bow and stern. This shoulder is formed by shaping planks from natural bends. No frames are inserted into the hull and the outrigger float and its connecting spars are of bamboo. A single spritsail is carried and steering is by quarter rudder. The most arresting feature of the *jukung*, however, is the prominent crutch in the stern in which mast and spars rest when not in use. This crutch is always made from a naturally grown crook with the arm terminating in some traditional carving such as a *wayang* or the like.

Albert Bickmore[7] who journeyed throughout Indonesian waters in 1865 provides an account of outrigger craft of that time. At Madura he saw *praus* each with 'a float on the leeward side while, on a kind of rack on the windward side was placed a canoe and everything on board that was movable.' The rack survives in the Sulawesi *sopé*, or *sekoci*, where there is one on each side of the hull.

Some of the *praus* that were seen by Bickmore at Madura must have been similar to the *golekan* but probably much more narrow in proportion to length and therefore in need of the stabilizing outrigger. His description of the triangular sails, with a single red or black cloth running through them adjacent to the leach could be applied to the sails of some other present-day craft throughout Indonesia particularly the *mayang* seining *prau* of West Java. They set a large single rectangular

Above and left: A marvel of Indonesian naval architecture. Fishing platforms at Sunda Kelapa, Jakarta. These have a single lateen sail and are steered by a rudder mounted in a central position on the aft cross-beam.

Right: *Jukungs* on the Rembang shore, Java. Hull planking is dowelled together and ribs are non-existent.

Right: A fishing *prau* at Cirebon. Here both sails are aft of the sprits but one would be drawing free when the *prau* sails 'on the wind'.

Far right, above: The *Gaya Baru*, a small *mayang* type of fishing *prau* of Cirebon. The mains'l is afoul of its sprit but the fores'l is drawing free as the *prau* enters harbour 'wing and wing'. A mizzen sail, with its spars, lies in a crutch.

Far right, below: The *jukung* has just gone about and those aboard have not yet settled down. In this view from astern the spritsail is shown to advantage and also the angle of the outrigger float attachment spar.

Left and below: A *jukung* on the beach at Rembang has a quaint *wayang* demon decorating the end of a crutch.

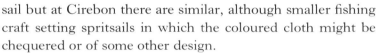

sail but at Cirebon there are similar, although smaller fishing craft setting spritsails in which the coloured cloth might be chequered or of some other design.

The *mayang*, or *majang*, *prau* with its canoe-like hull and prominent curved end pieces always brightly painted, sometimes in batik-like patterns, certainly provides a most colourful scene in an artist's paradise. But what is more important is that these diminutive craft, some nine meters long overall and little more than a meter in breadth amidships, make no small contribution to the vital needs of a community situated in one of the world's most densely populated areas. As the fishermen return to harbour during the day their catch is immediately auctioned in the roofed market nearby. These *praus* carry a crew of two but the larger seiners are said to have as many as twenty hands aboard when out fishing.

All these craft use the age-old single fluked 'pick' anchor made from wood. The shank fits tightly into a slot at one end of the arm so that there is an acute angle of about 35 degrees between the two parts. This angle is maintained with a length of rattan lashing from the shank to about half way along the arm. The anchor usually nestles over the starboard bow. Even in these *praus* there is a place for everything!

Besides the *jukungs* that are found all along the beautiful expanse of Rembang's shore there is a fleet of larger fishing craft that pull up on the beach right opposite the town. These are the *kontings* that rival even the Cirebon *praus* for the brilliance of their decorative paintwork. For that reason one is attracted to the *konting* as if it were a bird of paradise.

There is little variation in the size of any of Rembang's *kontings*. All of them measure about 25 feet overall. Their curving stems and stern-posts terminate in elongated shaped pieces cut off square at the head. In no other *prau* is there anything quite like them. In the bows, just abaft of the stem-head, and set at the same angle, are two prominent secondary posts. The only use I could see for them was to prevent the bamboo spars fouling the stem-head.

The sail set by the *konting* is rectangular and similar to that of the *mayang prau*—from a single pole mast, without any shrouds or stays. A quaint lantern for use on the fishing grounds is hung from the mast and nearby a large circular wooden tank is positioned to take the fish as they are caught so ensuring their freshness on arrival at the market.

Left: *Konting* anchors at Rembang.

Below right: The single-fluked wooden anchor keeps the *konting's* head facing seaward.

Below: A colourful fishing *prau* of Java is the *Konting*. These are at Rembang.

The painting of the *konting's* hull is a varied assortment of geometric patterns and curvilineal sweeps, these more especially in the vicinity of the bow and stern. The broad quarter rudder invariably comes in for its share of brushwork and when the artist has finished his work there he is likely to devote his attention to the mast.

My visit to Rembang coincided with the celebrations marking the end of Ramadan hence all the display of fringed flags, trimmings from spindly curved bamboos, tassels of coloured fibre and all manner of peculiar devices that give so much pleasure to Asian people during festive occasions. And what a fine sight one of these *praus* made as it romped along the coast with all its banners flying from slender bamboo wands and ornamental trimmings set from masts and spars.

Passing again the shore-bound craft I found it difficult to tear myself away from this wonderful scene that had not yet emerged from the age known to Marco Polo. Right alongside me were the wooden anchors of the *kontings*, bared by the receding sea, just as they have been for untold centuries.

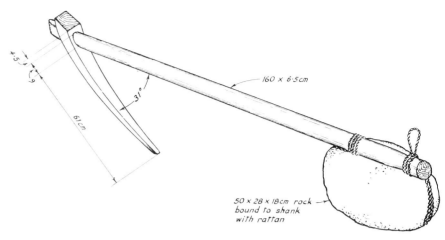

An Indonesian anchor.

Above: Windward and lee views of the *Bulan Purnama*. The helmsman is using the windward rudder.

Left: Pit-sawing timber at a Sulawesi *prau* yard. (Courtesy B. Leyland.)

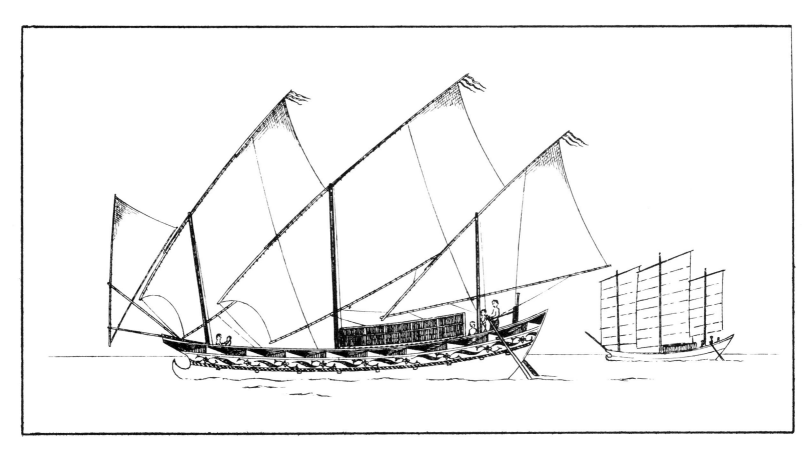

It was from Rembang that many of the biggest *praus* ever built came during the sixteenth century. These were the *jongs* that sometimes measured up to 700 tonnes to make the Portuguese *naus* small in comparison. They were built close to the sources of timber which in those times included Rembang, Japara and Cirebon on the north coast of Java. Not only were these towns great shipbuilding centres but also important ports whose vessels maintained foreign trade with countries as far distant as India and China.

The *jongs* were constructed in much the same manner as the present-day *praus*—with the planking edge-dowelled throughout. It is thought that the planks were also held together with mortices and tenons which were fastened with treenails driven through in an endeavour to give the big hulls greater strength. Sixteenth and seventeenth century illustrations of these craft show them as possessing peculiar upturned bows that resembled a form of bifid construction. A drawing by D'eerste Boeck, published in 1598, portrays a *jong* with a profusely decorated hull that must have been every bit as colourful as the *kontings* that I saw at Rembang only recently.

The largest *jong* in Boeck's drawing shows a tilted 'square' sail set from each of its two masts and a spritsail under a steeply angled bowsprit. But farther off there is a smaller *jong* setting lugsails similar in shape to those of the present-day Singapore trader. Unlike the sails of this vessel, however, those of the *jongs* were made from matting. That variations in rigs did

This reconstruction of a sixteenth century *jong* shows the *prau* carrying a combination of tilted 'square' sails and oceanic lateens. One of the latter is a headsail similar to that of a madura *leti-leti*. It is reasonable to suggest that such an arrangement was employed. No spritsail is shown under the bowsprit as the drawing represents a *jong* prior to the adoption of European-type sails. To leeward is another *jong* with the possible alternative rig of battened lugsails. It is assumed that the bows fanned out to form a 'V' transom.

The illustration is based on D'eerste Boek (1598) and Godinho de Eredia (1613); the indigenous sails of Indonesia and the decoration of the *konting*. Thwartship beams penetrate the planking as in the *golekan* and steering is by twin quarter rudders.

occur is confirmed by a drawing of a *jong* by Godinho de Erédia that was published in 1613, only a few years later than the Dutch illustration. Here the lugsails are shown lowered. Had they been set I am sure that their height would have far exceeded the width as was the case with the *praus* from Banda Aceh in Sumatra last century.

The masts of the *jong*, like those of the *golekan*, were stepped well forward with one in the bows and the other closer to amidships. It was not unusual for a short third mast to be stepped right aft. Indeed, the setting up of extra masts and larger or smaller sails according to the strength of the wind is the normal procedure for changing the sail area in *praus* that retain either the traditional lateen or tilted 'square' sails.

It hardly needs to be mentioned that steering in the *jongs* was performed with quarter rudders.

Left: In this canoe the sail is made of synthetic material.

Below left: A Sulawesi double canoe with twin oceanic lateen sails, partially furled. (Courtesy B. Leyland.)

Right: A rig similar to that of the Jakarta *kolek* is seen in this South Sulawesi outrigger canoe. (Courtesy B. Leyland.)

Below: This *kolek* in the Kali Besar has a quadrilateral spritsail. A smaller foresail can be set in the bows.

Above: The *pinisi Bunga Melati* at Sunda Kelapa.

Left: The modern *pinisi* with jib-headed sails. A topmast is stepped between the two main legs of the tripod main mast with its heel atop of the fore leg. The mizzen mast is a single spar.

Below: Aboard each *prau* in turn there is something of interest. A capstan, the bitts, a modern cabin and the 'midship structure of a *nadé*. Sunda Kelapa, looking south.

Right: In Jakarta's Kali Besar the smallest of the *koleks* mingle with the big ocean-going *praus*.

Above right: A double outrigger canoe off Ujung Pandang. An awning gives some shelter to the crew.

From Ship to Shore

Above: Madura trading *praus* crowd Jakarta's Kali Baru. The small craft are largely employed in punting cargo ashore and for ferrying ice and water.

Left: A gentle zephyr barely fills the sails of this timber-laden *pinisi*. A fine photograph by Adrian Horridge whose painstaking research on the *praus* has been recognised by the National Maritime Museum with the publication of his work in a number of monographs. (See Bibliography.)

The volume and nature of the Indonesian *prau* traffic is really astounding. Timber provides one of the main cargoes and in Sunda Kelapa *praus* from Sumatra crowd the Kali Besar as far as the eye can see disgorging load upon load of it direct into lorries or to be temporarily stacked on the quayside. Beyond, and out of sight, were other *praus* lined up at the canal entrance waiting for their turn to come in to a berth. Here the *praus* are either the two-masted *pinisi* or the single-masted *nadé*. At Kali Baru, however, although some of the *pinisi* and *nadé* are to be seen there, the majority of *praus* are the Madura *leti-leti* with an occasional *sekoci* or *golekan*.

There is no berthage for the *praus* at Kali Besar and no matter what the cargo is, whether timber, poles or coconuts, if not landed by way of a gangplank, must be rafted or ferried ashore. This congested haven must be very close to resembling a port in these parts well past a hundred years ago. There is no backdrop of modern buildings and cranes and forklifts are non-existent. Motor lorries are the only intrusion to spoil the illusion that one might be in another age.

Further east in Java, timber remains the predominant cargo but at Semarang and Surabaya it comes not from Sumatra but from Kalimantan. This is because the cross-winds, either from the east or west, are more suited to the *praus* operating under sail on this run. When a hold is crammed full more timber is stacked high on the deck until there is practically no freeboard. Many of the large *praus* now in commission are quite capable of stowing 200 tonnes below deck. I remember seeing timber so closely stowed that extracting the first planks and bringing them up through the small hatch was an extremely difficult task.

At Singapore I boarded the sloop rigged *Kota Baru* that had

Above: Flour being loaded into a *prau* at Sunda Kelapa. A workman rests in the shade of the delivery truck.

Left: Discharging Sumatran timber from a *pinisi* at Sunda Kelapa. The bilge pump can be seen immediately forward of the hatch.

Seamen out on the bowsprit of the *pinisi Cahaya Mutiara* are prepared to fend off other *praus* while making for a berth.

freighted some 100 tonnes of poles from her home port of Tanjung Pinang on Bintan (Kepulauan Riau). With a crew of eight, all from Tanjung Pinang, the *Kota Baru* had taken two days on the voyage. The *nakhoda*, Masud Sood, was also the *prau's* owner. He said that the freight on each pole was 0.70 Singapore dollars and the total receipts for the trip were shared between himself and the crew.

While general cargoes; household commodities and shipments of flour and cement; are made by *praus* out of Jakarta more varied cargoes that include bundles of rattan, kapok and other natural products of the eastern archipelago are landed at Surabaya. But the people of the outer islands are also caught up in the plastic age and not infrequently a *prau* will leave a Java port piled high with colourful manufactured goods from newly established industries.

While wandering through the shopping area of Ujung Pandang on the island of Sulawesi I came upon models of *praus*

Above: A small *prau pinisi* up for overhaul at Kali Baru, Jakarta. To the right is a *leti-leti*. The ice is being ferried to a fishing craft moored in the harbour.

Above right: The *Kota Baru* belongs to Tanjung Pinang in the Riau Islands. Mangrove poles are being discharged at Singapore.

Right: Small *praus* hauled out near Pare Pare. A close study of them would have entailed negotiating a not too healthy mangrove swamp.

that were made entirely from cloves. The sight of them took my mind back many years because that eminent Auckland shipbuilder, the late Charles Bailey Jnr., possessed such a model. He told me that it had come from Java and I have since seen one there myself, in Jakarta's Pasar Ikan. I believe these models are more readily available in the Moluccas—the Spice Islands—where the clove crop is more prolific. My delight in coming across them in the first instance on Sulawesi might well be imagined. Their hulls, masts, rigging, spars and sails (main and mizzen with gaff topsails, and three headsails), all consisting of strung cloves, so realistically represented as if billowing to a fine breeze. One model, measuring about 75 cm overall and 35 cm tall, was priced at 15,000 rupiahs, then approximately US$36.

Ujung Pandang is also known for its fine silver filigree jewelry and in the shops of the town will be found silver *praus* with sails far more delicately reproduced than any made from cloves. But the enterprising silversmiths in this thriving Makassarese centre of trade turn out anything and everything

to catch the eye, from butterflies to helicopters! Neither can the visitor avoid being approached by insistent vendors hawking real butterflies of sensational size and colouring. Touts also do their best to entice the unwary with the promise of a girl far more alluring than anything to be had in silver filigree.

Aboard a Bugis *pinisi* there is sometimes a member of the crew intent upon making a little extra money by whittling away at a piece of teak to produce a model of his seagoing home. Such models make fine curios and it is surprising how closely they resemble the real thing although one must necessarily make some allowance for 'modeller's licence'. In comparing a model with an actual *prau* the near accuracy of the miniature will be appreciated. The curvature of the combined keel, stem and stern-post well represented and masting and rigging true to life with shrouds, backstays and vangs all leading to their correct positions.

The very low age group of a *prau*'s crew seems to indicate that seafaring in these craft is not a lifelong occupation and that after but a few years at sea a *kelassi* has had his fill of working before the mast and wishes to come ashore. If, however, he should remain at sea to become thoroughly experienced in the handling of a *prau* a youth may eventually become a *nakhoda* although to gain such a position would depend on the recommendation of a *nakhoda*. Such a recommendation takes the place of any certificate granted through examination, either written or oral. It is not unusual for an owner or a part owner of a *prau* to be its *nakhoda* but an owner looks forward to the day when a son might have sufficient experience and the ability to succeed to the senior position in the *prau* while he retires to the shore, perhaps to set himself up as his own agent.

Above left: In port the deck of a *pinisi* becomes the focal point for both business and recreational activities with table and seating under an awning. The *nakhoda* of the *Cinta Usaha* sits cross-legged as young crew members display a model of their *prau*.

Left: A *pinisi* often has a modeller in its youthful crew. Although the rounded extremeties are typical of this type of *prau* they are somewhat exaggerated in this model.

Right: A pole-masted sloop with a built-up 'midship housing. The elevated poop is particularly noticeable in this *prau* at Sunda Kelapa. An improvised hoist serves as a means of going aloft in the absence of ratlines.

Above: The *Selat Pasam* from Sumatra has its *ambeng* built on logs that are only partially squared.

Left: The *Jamper Jaya*, an auxiliary sloop belonging to Surabaya, has a jib-headed mains'l furled in to the mast. On her port bow is a transom-sterned auxiliary ketch.

Above right: A sloop rigged *prau* from Jambi in Sumatra. A number of similar *praus* were seen in Sunda Kelapa's Kali Besar discharging timber. One, the *Pelita Abadi*, had a Japanese Kubota engine installed and a large deck house constructed aft. She carried 114 tonnes on a 3 meter draught.

Near right, below: The *nadé Baco Neranti* sets a jib-headed mains'l and an expansive stays'l. The unobstructed deck allows a large timber cargo to be carried.

Far right, below: The single-masted *nadé*, has a cabin built over the hold. The brails for taking in the mains'l are clearly seen.

Prau Layar Motor

Above: While still in service this *prau* is being converted to a motor vessel with the addition of a navigation house and bridge deck.

Left: A *pinisi* with a prominent deck house aft.

We are constantly reminded of the changes that have taken place in the *praus* and their trade, particularly during recent times. And now the impact of mechanization is very much in evidence with more and more *praus* abandoning sail as their principal means of propulsion.

Ever since the appearance of European vessels in the Indies *praus* have absorbed certain characteristics from them and the process of change is continuing. Some hulls are an admixture of European and Indonesian construction while the fore-and-aft rig is commonplace. Unlike the Arabs, however, Indonesian *prau* owners have been much slower to appreciate the advantages of auxiliary power. But suddenly the change is taking place and a visit to Sunda Kelapa, at any time, will reveal an ever increasing number of *praus* being engined and having wheel houses and even bridge decks added.

Originally *praus* were double-ended as were the *dhows*. Portuguese influence resulted in the transom sterns of the Arab *sambuk*, *baghla* and *ganja* and also of the Indian *kotia*. The influence then spread to the Indies where the transom stern has experienced probably over four centuries of evolution to attain its present form in the *pinisi*. The transom stern has by no means been universally accepted though and the traditional double-ended hull, and lateen rig, is retained in numerous types of *prau*. Perhaps the finest example of this individualism is seen in the *golekan* of Madura which continues to set the oceanic lateen sails between bamboo spars and trail a quarter rudder.

A *prau* that appears to have become popular in the Banda Sea area, especially in the vicinity of Ambon, is the *lambok* (or *lambo*). These vessels, more European in character than Indonesian, are an odd-looking lot, usually having a counter

stern and straight stem. A peculiarity is the 'midship housing over the hold although this also appears in certain other *praus* right through to Sumatra. The *lambok* is ketch rigged and the single headsail extends to the end of an ungainly tripartite bowsprit. Gibson-Hill remarked that the best *lamboks* came from Bonerate, an island to the south of Sulawesi which accounts for these vessels being seen in Ujung Pandang.

Far more pleasing to the eye than the *lambok* is the single-masted Sulawesi *nadé* which has a hull similar to that of the *pinisi*. Some are cutter-rigged with gaff tops'l and perhaps two headsails while others have adopted the jib-headed mains'l. There is also a Sumatran *nadé* many of which are engaged in freighting timber to Java from Jambi and the Palembang area. The hull of this *prau*, however, has such a pronounced flare that it must be an extremely tender craft without any cargo aboard. They usually carry a jib-headed loose-footed mains'l and an enormous stays'l set on a bamboo boom that reaches out to the end of the tripartite sprit. These are *praus* that oft times have the 'midship housing over the hold like that in the *lambok*. Its sides are only a short distance inboard and the roofing or decking above is usually more or less level, rarely taking on the sheer of the main deck. Timber can be stowed right to the top of this housing and all of it is manhandled through an opening in its fore end. Due to the manner in which the *praus* berth, bow on to the shore and with a plank thrown over the side as a gangway, this forward access to the hold is most convenient for the handling of timber cargoes, every length of which is loaded and discharged without any mechanical aid. The hold can also

Far left, above: The *lambok* ketch. (Courtesy B. Leyland.)

Near left, above: The *lambok* from the lee quarter. (Courtesy B. Leyland.)

Below left: *Praus* discharging timber in the Kali Besar, Sunda Kelapa (looking north). The nearer vessel has been converted to a *prau layar motor*.

Above: Some *praus* have a cabin-like structure built right across the main deck, as in this *nadé*.

be entered through the housing from aft. There is no deck within although the beams that support the main deck out in the open do pass completely through the interior of the housing.

More *praus* of the *pinisi* and *nadé* types are now dispensing with quarter rudders in favour of one hung from a slanting stern-post. In such cases the post penetrates the *ambeng* and the tiller is entirely within the low cabin. There the helmsman stands poking his head through an opening, or scuttle, for a clear view forward.

Some *nadé* are as big as the largest *pinisi* and carry an enormous timber cargo stowed below and on deck. With the cabin within the *ambeng* poop structure cantilevered out over the stern practically the whole of the main deck can be devoted to the stowing of timber. The accommodation for the crew is of secondary importance as indicated by its siting for surely even the Java Sea can become sufficiently rough at times to carry such structures away.

It might be said that the timber carrying *praus* are performing a similar task in Indonesia as that of the New Zealand scow some years ago. The *prau's* loading, though, is probably far greater in comparison because of the absence of the stringent regulations that applied to the scows. In Indonesia there is a *prau* owners' association but no union to protect the interests of the seamen who see no danger in their occupation and are quite happy anyway!

While ascertaining the names of various *praus* I was most puzzled by the use of the prefix PLM, more particularly in the *prau pinisi*. There was the *P.L.M. Buana Rakhmat* of Surabaya, the *P.L.M. Budi Agung* of Ujung Pandang and the *P.L.M. Ambologo*, again from Surabaya. After making many comparisons and putting two and two together it was finally confirmed that what had baffled me was the result of modernization. Vessels that bear the initials PLM are none other than *Praus Layar Motor*—motor sailing *praus*.

Above: The acme of modern *prau* design. The *Fajar Harapan* with a canoe (cruiser) stern, navigation bridge and bipod main mast. The mizzen could serve no useful purpose but tradition dies hard. Out of character with this modernization is the retention of the quarter rudders.

Right: In the style of a 19th century clipper ship the stem of the *pinisi Sinar Tarasu* dare not be adorned with a figurehead but a scroll would not go amiss.

Types of Trading Praus

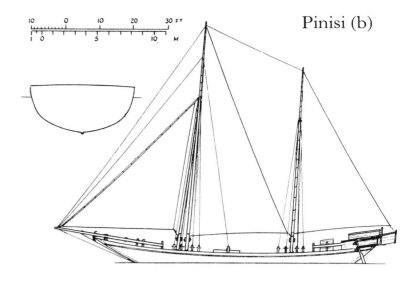

Pinisi (b)

Pinisi (a)

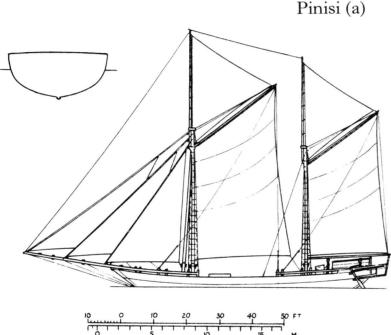

The *pinisi* is a *prau* that is constantly changing with the times. There is now a tendency to fit it out with jib-headed sails which are easier to handle than the gaff sails. A large single heads'l eliminates the long bowsprit which is vulnerable to damage both at sea and in a crowded *pelabuhan*. The tripod fore or mainmast is usually retained with the topmast stepped within the head of the structure. The mizzen is more often than not a single spar.

There are many variations in both of the main classes of *pinisi* and canoe and transom sterns are encountered. A single hung rudder sometimes takes the place of quarter rudders. Hulls and masting are predominantly white or light blue and only occasionally red.

The *pinisi* is easily recognized by its ketch rig with standing gaffs. The hull is also quite distinctive, bulging out to an extreme 'midship breadth of approximately one third of the water line length. There is a flush deck rising gradually to the bows but steeply towards the high sloping poop. A tripartite bowsprit and bipod mainmast stepped in tabernacles are features of this *prau*. Nowadays the mizzen is either bipod or a single mast. It is customary for batten 'ladders' to be run up to the cross trees. These are attached to the shrouds although they do not always appear on both sides of a mast and sometimes they are absent altogether.

Sails are usually tanned brown or dark blue and are brailed in to the masts. Quarter rudders are lashed in recesses in the 'thwartship beams, one above the other, and are unshipped while the *prau* is in port. The *pinisi* forms the bulk of the *prau* traffic in the Java Sea.

Lambok

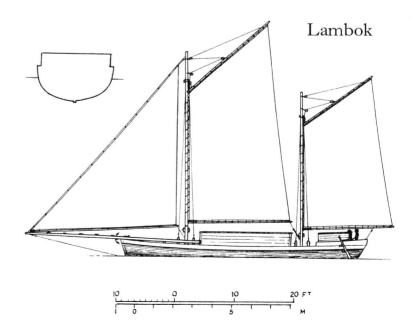

128

The *lambok* is an odd craft in the *prau* world and is mainly European in character. It is more likely to be seen in the Moluccas and many centre on Ambon to form a heterogenous collection of ketch rig. Although pole masts are stepped the tripartite bowsprit is retained over a straight but slightly angled stem. There is usually an enormous boomed staysail from the end of the sprit and the main is a gaff sail. A prominent rectangular housing is built in the waist of the hull enclosing the hold. To add to this ungainliness there is either a crude counter or transom stern. Despite such attempts at Europeanization quarter rudders persist.

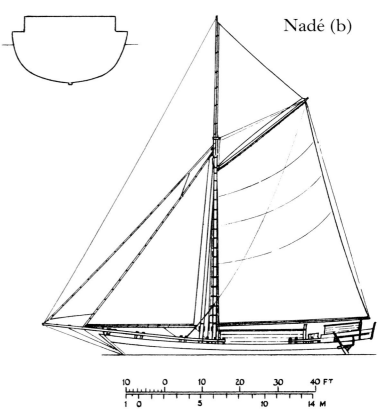

Nadé (b)

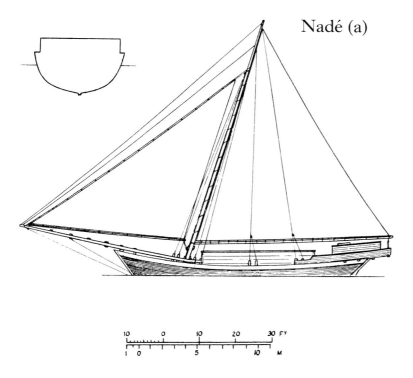

Nadé (a)

This cutter-rigged *nadé* with a gaff topsail is from Sulawesi and is actually a single-masted version of the *pinisi*. There is little difference in hull form apart from its smaller size. As with the former *prau* there is a cabin built over the hold. The *ambeng* or poop is similar to that in the ketch-rigged *pinisi* and steering is by quarter rudders. The traditional tripod form of masting is retained as is the tripartite bowsprit. Paintwork too is like that of the *pinisi*—predominantly light blue and white although red is not unknown.

At least three main types of *nadé* exist but the jib-headed sloop is the one that is most numerous especially in Sumatra and Java. Some from Riau and the north of Sumatra are open waisted and are gunter rigged but those engaged in the timber trade from Sumatra to Java have their hold built up with a cabin over the entire 'midship section of the hull. There is no deck within although beams at deck level continue throughout. In section the hull has a pronounced flare and there is great sheer forward. A wide *ambeng* is cantilevered over the stern and often this is supported by very roughly fashioned logs. Accommodation for the crew is frugal and has only sufficient height to crouch in. Steering is with a normal rudder and the helmsman operates the tiller from within the cabin with his head poking through an open hatch.

Hulls and masts are usually painted red but some *nadé* are devoid of any paint at all.

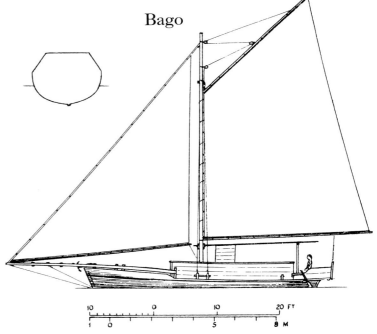

Bago

The *bago* is not a particularly attractive *prau*. The hull possesses a straight but slightly sloping stem and stern-post. The large cabin with angled sides and flat roof extends from forward of the mast to a position adjacent to the 'thwartship beam that supports the quarter rudder. The *ambeng* is plain and box-like and looks as if it might be an afterthought. A pole mast is erected in a tabernacle on top of the cabin. The gaff mains'l is not gathered in to the mast with brails but is lowered with its gaff. The expansive staysail has a bamboo spar at its foot and this reaches right to the end of the tripartite sprit. This *prau* can be seen in Java but is better known towards Bali and the islands to the east.

Golekan (a)

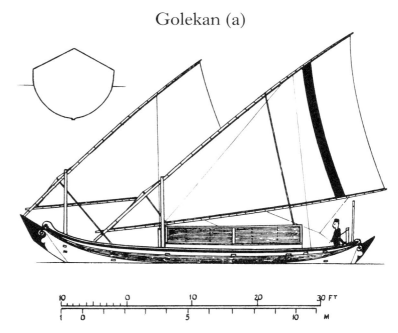

The Madura *golekan* is a distinctive *prau* with deep 'V' stem and stern pieces adorned with intricate floral patterns. On the sides of these prominent end pieces is a black-painted area separated from the rest of the hull by a scroll border. This form of decor is typical of the Madura *prau*. The upper strakes, in which there is considerable sheer, are painted in various hues of brown and chromes.

From stump masts lateen sails are set between laminated bamboo spars. These are hung at a point very close to their foot so that it is necessary to provide additional support to the yard in the form of a prop. Vangs are taken to the end of an outrigger boom. A feature of the hull is the projection of the 'thwartship beams throughout its length. Into a slot in the ends of these beam ends a wedge is driven thereby locking the sides of the hull together.

Pajala

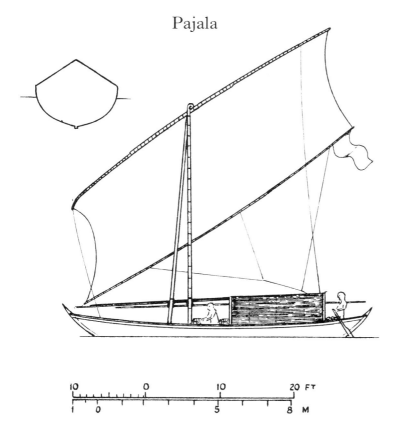

The *pajala* is a double-ended undecked *prau* that might very well be likened to an incompletely planked up *palari* or *patorani*. The addition of another strake on each side together with terminating bulkheads or transoms would completely change the character of this craft. But never mind, this is one of the *praus* from Sulawesi that continues to set the traditional tilted 'square' sail or *sombala tanja* between bamboo spars. The tripod masting is also constructed from bamboos set up in tabernacles.

Here we see the split bamboo and *atap* shelter that gives so many of the Indonesian craft that 'native' look. Steering, as might be expected, is by quarter rudders.

Golekan (b)

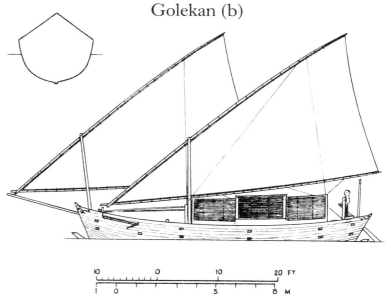

The *golekan* in an earlier form continues to give faithful service in the freighting of logs, poles and timber to the ports of Java. These *praus* are the largest to have bifid bows and sterns and for this reason alone they are worthy of close study. The projections are upturned extensions of the keel and when the *prau* is fully laden they just break the surface of the sea. The hulls possess wide 'V' transoms at both bow and stern. They are profusely decorated with foliated panels, incised and painted more generally in blues and browns. Decorative paintwork also extends, in varying patterns entirely foreign to any other craft, along the sides of the hull and in some instances on the keel projections too. The main body of the hull is a well weathered dirty brown. Some fine examples of ship-carving appear in some of these *golekans*, notably in the Indonesian equivalent of catheads, ends of booms and crutches. Again beams penetrate through the hull planking. There is no deck under the shelter amidships. Instead there is a 'thwartship platform of split bamboo right aft on which the crew can rest.

Leti-leti

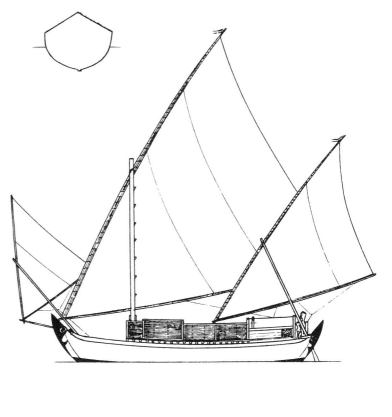

Patorani

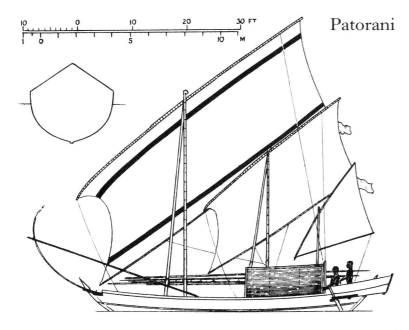

The *patorani* of southern Sulawesi is one of the older types of *prau*. It retains the bamboo tripod masting and the tilted 'square' sails. The masts terminate in curled-over heads and the two 'thwartship legs of the mainmast are neatly bound at regular intervals with rattan. Sails are of light cotton and sometimes they are printed with light blue or green vertical stripes or there is a black cloth inserted near the leach or alternatively there is a black strip at the head of the mains'l and another at the foot.

The hull of the *patorani* has a high curved stem and stern-post to match. *Palari*-type end transoms provide a low area in the bows. This is repeated in the stern but it is hidden from view by the *ambeng*. There are twin quarter rudders.

The *leti-leti* is a solidly built *prau* from Madura. It can be either single or two masted with oceanic lateen sails. The mizzen is usually stepped right in the stern and cants forward to lean on the cabin end. In some vessels, however, this mast is stepped upright at the fore end of the cabin. The stout main-mast has wedge-shaped treads to give access aloft. The main-yard is a fine spar made up from a number of selected bamboos but the mizzen-yard, serving a smaller sail, is of much lighter construction and from fewer bamboos. From still lighter spars an even smaller lateen is set over the bows. This serves as a substitute for a staysail.

Ridged roofing with panels of split bamboo is built over the hold. It is possible to slide back the section of this roofing immediately aft of the mainmast. Adjoining the 'midship roofing is a fully-timbered cabin for the crew. There is then just sufficient room left for the helmsman to operate the well-proportioned quarter rudder. It should be explained that the angle of these rudders is maintained by a rope, one end of which is attached to the head of the rudder and the other to a stanchion set up in a central position a little abaft of the helmsman. There is no *ambeng* or bowsprit in the *leti-leti*.

Sekoci

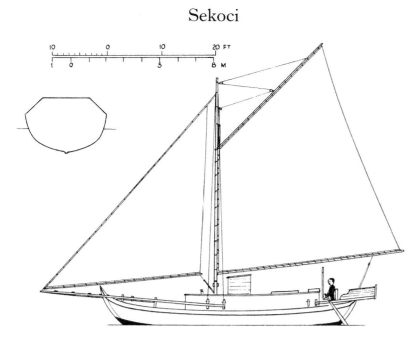

The *sekoci* is another queer craft of mixed heritage—partly Indonesian and partly European. The hull is very similar in construction to that of the *leti-leti* but has a longer and more pointed stem and stern post. There is a long cabin structure with sloping sides and a flat roof built over the greater part of the hold. The firebox is placed on top of the cabin as there is little room elsewhere for it. There is also access to the hold through a hatch in the roofing. Unlike the *leti-leti* there is an *ambeng* over the stern and a tripartite sprit forward.

The *sekoci* is a gaff-rigged sloop with the mast stepped in a tabernacle atop of the forward end of the cabin. As in the *bago* the headsail is on a bamboo spar that spans the whole distance between the end of the sprit and the mast.

Addendum

HULL CONSTRUCTION. The remark by Stavorinus (p. 41) that 'in Europe we build reversely' to Indonesian practise by setting up the frame first would not be entirely correct. In Scandinavia planking up first and then inserting the ribs has been customary even during the present century.

Refer: Olof Hasslöf *The Technology of Ship-building in Ships and Shipyards, Sailors and Fishermen,* Copenhagen University Press 1972.

THE *JUKUNG*. The term *jukung* extends to the Cocos Islands where there is a small open boat of that name measuring from ten to twelve feet in length and gunter rigged.

Refer: Cocos I. 35c postage stamp issued 1976.

THE *JONG*. For almost a hundred years Malays in and about Singapore have sailed model outrigger *koleks* known as *jongs*. They are usually raced in two classes according to size. The largest of these *jongs* measure approximately $6\frac{1}{2}$ feet in length and the smallest about half that size. They carry a jib-headed mains'l and a boomed heads'l. The outrigger is connected to the main hull by a single spar and a short vertical connective piece.

Refer: *Straits Times Annual*, Singapore 1979.

Bibliography

ADMIRALTY. *Fishing and Trading Craft of the Netherlands East Indies, New Guinea and the Solomon Islands*, London 1944

BLAKE, W. M. *The Madura Proa*, Yachting, Jan. 1929
 Another Bugis Sailing Craft, Yachting, March 1929

COLLINS, G. E. P. *East Monsoon*, Scribners, New York, 1937
 Makassar Sailing, Jonathan Cape, London 1937
 Seafarers of South Celebes, National Geographic, Washington, Vol. 87, No. 1, Jan. 1945.
 With Malays at Sea, Geographic Magazine, London, March 1937

DICK, H. W. *Proa Shipping in Eastern Indonesia*, Bulletin of Indonesian Economic Studies, Canberra, Vol. XI, No. 2; Vol. XI, No. 3. July & Nov. 1975

FORREST, T. *A Voyage to New Guinea and the Moluccas from Balambangan*, London, 1779

GIBSON-HILL, C. A. *The Indonesian Boats Reaching Singapore*, J.M.B.R.A.S.,* Vol. XXIII, Pt. 1, Feb. 1950
 Cargo Boats of the East Coast of Malaya, J.M.B.R.A.S.,* Vol. XXII, Pt. III, June 1949
 The Origin of the Trengganu Pinas, J.M.B.R.A.S.,* Vol. XXVI, Pt. I, July 1953
 Tonkang and Lighter Matters, J.M.B.R.A.S,* Vol. XXV, Pt. 1, Aug. 1952

HOBMAN, R. J. *The Creation of Siola Tau*, The Wooden Boat, U.S.A. No. 10, May–June 1976

HORRIDGE, G. A. *The Konjo Boatbuilders and the Bugis Prahus of South Sulawesi*, National Maritime Museum Monograph No. 40, Greenwich
 The Lambo or Prahu Bot: A Wooden Ship in an Eastern Setting, National Maritime Museum Monograph No. 39, Greenwich, 1979
 The Design of Planked Boats of the Moluccas, National Maritime Museum Monograph No. 38, Greenwich, 1978

MACKNIGHT, C. C. *Courted by the Winds*, Hemisphere, Asian-Australian Monthly, Vol. XXI, No. 8, 1978
 The Farthest Coast, Melbourne University Press, 1969

The Macassans: a study of the early trepang industry along the Northern Territory coast. Ph.D. thesis, A.N.U., Canberra, 1969
The Sea Voyagers of Eastern Indonesia, Hemisphere, Vol. XIII, No. 4, April 1969
The Voyage to Marege, Melbourne University Press, 1976
The Study of Praus in the Indonesian Archipelago, I.C.I.O.S.,** Perth, 1979
The Nature of Early Maritime Trade, World Archaeology, London, Vol. 5, No. 2, Oct. 1973

MACKNIGHT & THORNE, A. G. *Two Macassan Burials in Arnheim Land*. Archaeology & Physical Anthropology in Oceania, Vol. 3, No. 3, Oct. 1968

MANGUIN, P. *The Southeast Asian Trading Ship. An Historical Approach*, I.C.I.O.S.,** Perth, 1979

MORRIS, J. *The Hasans: A Buginese Trading Family* (film), Film Australia, Lindfield, N.S.W.

RAFFLES, S. *The Maritime Code of the Malays*, J.S.B.R.A.S.,*** July 1879

ROONEY, J. *The Makassar Ketch*, The Wooden Boat, U.S.A. No. 14, Jan.–Feb. 1977

STAVORINUS, J. S. *Voyages to the East Indies*, London, 1798

* *Journal Malayan Branch Royal Asiatic Society*
** *International Conference on Indian Ocean Studies (paper)*
*** *Journal Singapore Branch Royal Asiatic Society*

Footnotes

1. Minister of Transport, Communications & Tourism, Jakarta.
2. G. Collins, *Makassar Sailing.*
3. Capt. W. C. Lennon.
4. G. W. Earl.
5. *A Voyage to New Guinea and the Moluccas.*
6. *Water Transport.*
7. *Travels in the Indian Archipelago.*

Index

Note : Numbers printed in bold refer to illustrations